A FRIENDLY GUIDE TO
THE RESURRECTION OF JESUS

FRANCIS J MOLONEY SDB

garratt PUBLISHING

Published in Australia by
Garratt Publishing
32 Glenvale Crescent
Mulgrave, Vic. 3170

www.garrattpublishing.com.au

Copyright © Francis J Moloney sdb 2016

All rights reserved. Except as provided by the Australian copyright law, no part of this book may be reproduced in any way without permission in writing from the publisher.

Illustrations by Shane Conroy
Design and typesetting by Lynne Muir

Scripture quotations are drawn from the *New Revised Standard Version of the Bible*, copyright © 1989 by the Division of Christian Education of the National Council of the Churches of Christ in the USA.

Used by permission.
All rights reserved.

Nihil Obstat: Reverend Monsignor Peter J Kenny STD, Diocesan Censor
Imprimatur: Monsignor Greg Bennet, Vicar General
Date: 5 August 2016

The Nihil Obstat and Imprimatur are official declarations that a book or pamphlet is free of doctrinal or moral error. No implication is contained therein that those who have granted the Nihil Obstat and Imprimatur agree with the contents, opinions or statements expressed. They do not necessarily signify that the work is approved as a basic text for catechetical instruction.

ISBN 9781925073171
Cataloguing in Publication information for this title is available from the National Library of Australia. www.nla.gov.au

The author and publisher gratefully acknowledge the permission granted to reproduce the copyright material in this book. Every effort has been made to trace copyright holders and to obtain their permission for the use of copyright material.

The publisher apologises for any errors or omissions in the above list and would be grateful if notified of any corrections that should be incorporated in future reprints or editions of this book.

CONTENTS

NOTE FROM THE AUTHOR	3
NOTES ON THE ARTWORK	3
INTRODUCTION	4

CHAPTER ONE:
THE EARLIEST WITNESSES — 8
- Primitive Confessions of Faith — 8
- 1 Corinthians 15:3-8 — 9

CHAPTER TWO:
THE GOSPELS: BORN IN THE RESURRECTION — 12

CHAPTER THREE:
THE GOSPEL OF MARK — 15
- Women at the Tomb — 16
- The Easter Proclamation — 16
- Failure — 17
- Promises fulfilled — 18

CHAPTER FOUR:
THE GOSPEL OF MATTHEW — 19
- Women at the Tomb — 20
- The Guard's Report — 21
- Commissioning — 21
- At the end of the age — 23

CHAPTER FIVE:
THE GOSPEL OF LUKE — 26
- Women at the Tomb — 27
- The Journey to Emmaus — 28
- Commissioning — 30
- Ascension — 31
- To the ends of the earth — 31

CHAPTER SIX:
TWO STORIES IN THE GOSPEL OF JOHN — 32
JOHN 20 — 33
- Mary Magdalene, Simon Peter, and the Beloved Disciple — 33
- The Beloved Disciple's Journey of Faith — 33
- Mary Magdalene's Journey of Faith — 34
- Commissioning — 35
- Thomas' Journey of Faith — 35
- The First Conclusion — 36
- Believing without seeing — 36

A MAJOR FEAST DAY FOR MARY MAGDALENE — 37

JOHN 21 — 38
- A Fishing Miracle — 39
- Peter and the Beloved Disciple — 40
- John's Second Conclusion — 42
- A new commandment — 42

CHAPTER SEVEN:
WHAT HAPPENED? — 43
- The Empty Tomb — 43
- The Appearances — 44
- God is at work — 44

CHAPTER EIGHT:
WHAT DOES THE RESURRECTION OF JESUS MEAN? — 45
- For Jesus — 45
- For Jesus' Followers — 45
- We live in the faith — 46

REFERENCES — 48

ABOUT THE ARTIST

Shane Conroy is an Australian artist living in Mexico and a former Art Director for Dove Communications in the early 1980s. He designed the award-winning publication 'Woman: First Among the Faithful' by Frank Moloney in 1985.

Note from the Author

For some years Garratt Publishing has issued a series of books under the rubric of *A Friendly Guide*. They have proved to be extremely helpful, and point to the urgent need for the Catholic Church to respond to the exhortations of the Second Vatican Council, and Church leadership since then: *to recognise that the Word of God must be at the centre of Christian life and practice*. Although a number of the books have been dedicated to issues central to the life of the Catholic Church (Prayer, the Mass, Vatican II), the majority have focused upon the Word of God (the Old Testament, the Prophets, the New Testament, Jesus, the Gospels of Mark, Matthew, Luke, and John, and the Letters of Paul). This series speaks directly to the non-specialist reader, is attractively designed, and each brief volume provides up-to-date information in an easily digestible bite-size. I trust what follows continues that tradition.

The present volume, *A Friendly Guide to the Resurrection of Jesus*, reflects upon the very foundation of the Christian Tradition. Although its major interest is in the witness of the earliest Church to the resurrection, it also asks what happened, and what those inspired witnesses might say to Christians today. Much of what follows is guided by my *The Resurrection of the Messiah. A Narrative Commentary on the Resurrection Accounts in the Four Gospels* (Mahwah/New York: Paulist Press, 2013). The biblical text used is the NRSV translation, except for a few places where I have offered my own translation. That is always indicated with the abbreviation AT (author's translation). This *Friendly Guide* attempts to reach all Christians who accept that the resurrection of Jesus is the bedrock of their Christian faith, life, and practice. This message retains its power and continues to give meaning to what we hold dear.

Francis J. Moloney, SDB, AM, FAHA
Australian Catholic University,
Melbourne, Victoria, Australia

Notes on the Artwork

"The artwork for this book encompasses many symbols of the resurrection.

The ancient Palm (palmette) symbol has a very direct relationship to Christ and was used by the ancient Egyptians, the Greeks, the Romans and in India.

So too was the lotus, seen since ancient times as a symbol of resurrection and renewal because it closes with the dark and opens with the sunrise, growing with great beauty from the mud of the lake.

The illustration on page 48 features the symbol of Constantine's Chi Rho with Jesus as Christ the light. The signs 'alpha' and 'omega' signify the beginning and the end.

Around Jesus are significant people represented in the Gospels showing their feelings of awe; the two women at the tomb, the young man, two disciples and Peter bringing bread to the table. The fishermen who witnessed the miracle of the fish are also represented.

Shane says: "Apart from imagining the awe that the apostles and the others must have experienced, I tried to contemplate what Jesus himself must have experienced almost impossible to imagine his joy. I have tried to put the focus on the experiences/reactions of the 'witnesses' rather than on the image of Jesus. (Thats why he is there in the middle but with his back to us too)."

The whole image is surrounded by a mosaic type border common from ancient Roman days.

Introduction

Practising Christians take it for granted that Jesus of Nazareth was crucified and subsequently, after three days, raised by God from the dead. This certainty is not shared by millions of people who belong to other religious traditions, or who have no religious commitment.

Our secularised world, outstandingly represented by contemporary Australian culture, regards such claims by Christians as unrealistic; people simply do not rise from the dead.

For the ancients, rhythms of nature (the stars, the moon, the seasons of the year, and the cycle of plant life) are marked by birth, life, death, burial, and rebirth. Is it possible that Christianity has adopted some of those ancient "myths" that explain the world and its cycles and applied it to Jesus of Nazareth?

Many have made this suggestion, respecting Christianity, but not on the basis of the physical resurrection of its founder. Some modern critical scholarship, even on the basis of the New Testament evidence itself, argues that the proclamation of Jesus' resurrection was inspired by an ongoing experience of Jesus within the community, not by a physical phenomenon. But the physical resurrection of Jesus remains a pillar of Christian faith. As St Paul stated in 54 CE: "If Christ has not been raised, then our proclamation has been in vain and your faith has been in vain" (1 Cor 15:14).

The pages that follow are not written *to convince* others that Jesus was indeed raised by God, but *to affirm* the depth and the beauty of Christian belief in the resurrection of Jesus. I am fully aware of the complex nature of the early Church's description and understanding of Jesus' departure from the human stage. Among Christians, however, the rich historical, literary, and theological complexity surrounding the first expressions [of the resurrection] in the pages of the New Testament receives too little attention. We just state what we believe and ask no further questions. We need to go further. Although the historical reality of an empty tomb deserves our attention, belief in the resurrection is founded upon the faith of the earliest Church, not a hole in the ground.

That witness is not very concerned with *what happened to Jesus*. The earliest Christians took it for granted that God entered the life and death of Jesus, with unconditional acceptance of Jesus' radical obedience to his Father. God raised Jesus of Nazareth from the dead. As we will see, all the earliest confessions of faith in the resurrection of Jesus affirm this truth: God raised Jesus. While we traditionally say: "Jesus rose from the dead," the earliest witnesses claim: "*God raised Jesus from the dead.*" The resurrection of Jesus is a world-questioning action of God that took place in history, even though it defies history. On the basis of that unshakeable belief, the earliest Christians proclaimed, in their preaching (St Paul) and in their narratives (the Gospels of Mark, Matthew, Luke, and John), *what happened to the believers because of Jesus' resurrection.*

The *Friendly Guide to the Resurrection of Jesus* will trace the historical development of the early Church's confession of faith in the resurrection of Jesus. Prior to the life, teaching, and death of Jesus of Nazareth, the question of belief in the resurrection from the dead has an interesting history. For centuries Jewish writings show little or no interest in an afterlife. God's blessings were reflected in the prosperity of a life well-lived (Psalms 16:9-10; 73:23-26; 104:27-30; Mal 3:13-21). In the centuries immediately prior to Jesus, as Israel experienced suffering and subordination to powerful nations, the idea of an afterlife emerged. Why do the good suffer, and the wicked prosper? For some an afterlife would be a restoration of the dead person's physical condition (2 Macc 7:1-42), for others it would be a more spiritual experience (Wisdom 3:1-9). Jesus of Nazareth and the earliest Church accepted this new Jewish doctrine: there would be a life after death. The nature of that life would be determined by the quality of a person's life before death (Mark 12:18-27; Matt 22:23-33; Luke 20:27-38). For all the versatility this developing Jewish doctrine had in the time of Jesus, *it does not concern us.* **The resurrection of Jesus is not about the possibility of life after death. It is about the belief that a man who was cruelly executed, and buried, was experienced as alive, witnessed to by many.**

Our earliest witnesses come from the time before St Paul, who wrote across the 50s of the first Christian century. We have them because they came to life as brief exclamations and confessions of faith in the resurrection that have been incorporated into later documents. They come from the first years of the existence of a believing Christian community. From there we turn to examine Paul's recalling the central place of the resurrection of Jesus for the community at Corinth, found in 1 Corinthians 15:3-8. Remarkably, Paul shows little concern for the events that marked Jesus' life and ministry. No doubt he was aware of them, but at this early stage of the life of the Christian community, and in its preaching, he focuses entirely upon the saving significance of the death and resurrection of Jesus.

"We proclaim Christ crucified, a stumbling block to Jews and foolishness to Gentiles, but to those

> Our secularised world, outstandingly represented by contemporary Australian culture, regards such claims by Christians as unrealistic; people simply do not rise from the dead.

For the ancients, rhythms of nature (the stars, the moon, the seasons of the year, and the cycle of plant life) are marked by birth, life, death, burial, and rebirth. Is it possible that Christianity has adopted some of those ancient "myths" that explain the world and its cycles, and applied it to Jesus of Nazareth?

who are called, both Jews and Greeks, Christ the power of God and the wisdom of God" (1 Cor 1:23-24).

Writing in 54 CE, Paul reminds the Corinthians of something he taught them, but which he himself received in 1 Corinthians 15:3-8. We are dealing with a very ancient witness to the resurrection faith of the Church, earlier than Paul's conversion, which most likely took place in early 30 CE. It was not until about 70 CE that the earliest Gospel writer (the Gospel of Mark) began to "tell a story" about the resurrection. This story was retold in what later came to be accepted as the Christian Scriptures by the Gospels of Matthew and Luke (in late 80 CE), and eventually in the Gospel of John (about 100 CE).

Nourished by this rich reflection upon the faith that was born of the resurrection of Jesus, expressed through our inspired Sacred Scriptures, we will then be in a position to ask some questions about what we can discover about what happened on that first Easter morning, and what the resurrection of Jesus means for us today. We cannot be sure of the exact names of all of the authors behind the writings of earliest Christianity. There is no doubt that Paul of Tarsus, an earlier persecutor of Christians and one of its most creative theologians, wrote the First Letter to the Corinthians. The names given to the authors of the

> "We proclaim Christ crucified, a stumbling block to Jews and foolishness to Gentiles, but to those who are called, both Jews and Greeks, Christ the power of God and the wisdom of God" (1 Cor 1:23-24).

Gospels became part of the tradition late in the second century, as the Four Gospels were described as "according to" Mark, Matthew, Luke and John.

This step was taken because of the tendency, at that time, to compose a life of Jesus that "blended" all four Gospels. That tendency had to be resisted, as Christians understood that each of the Evangelists told the story *in a different way*. **Each of these inspired, but different, stories of Jesus enrich our understanding of who Jesus was, and what God has done for us in and through him. So it will always be, as we respond to the challenge of our Risen Lord. Each Easter we proclaim, along with the Greek-speaking Church: "Christ has been raised!" (Christos anēsti!), and respond "He has been raised indeed!" (Alēthōs anēsti!).**

A famous twentieth-century scholar (Rudolf Bultmann) once said that Jesus rises again and again in that proclamation. Many rejected his claim, as it revealed a deep scepticism about the historical fact of the resurrection of Jesus. But his suggestion contains an important element of truth: in our Easter proclamation we recognise the "truth" of the fundamental claim of the Christian tradition: Jesus, our Lord, is alive and among us.

SUMMING UP

✛ From its first days the Christian communities affirmed that Jesus had been raised by God.

✛ Paul does not tell the "story of Jesus", but focuses intensely upon the significance of the death and the resurrection of Jesus.

✛ The early Church did not proclaim that Jesus had risen, but that God has raised Jesus.

✛ The major concern of the Gospel narratives about the resurrection is what the event meant for the disciples, rather than what it meant for Jesus.

Chapter One
The Earliest Witnesses

It is sometimes thought that Paul was the earliest witness to the Christian tradition. Paul is certainly the author of the earliest *written* documents that we have in our New Testament. But he was initially a persecutor of the Christians (Gal 1:13, 23; Phil 3:6; 1 Cor 15:9).

The intervention of God led him to recognise that Jesus of Nazareth's death and resurrection had created an entirely new possibility for all humankind (Rom 5:12-21). Paul was overwhelmed by "the power of his resurrection" (Phil 3:10, Gal 1:13-24; Phil 3:7-11;1 Cor 1:18; 2 Cor 4:7; 12:9; 13:4). This experience is recounted three times in the Acts of the Apostles (Acts 9:1-30; 22:3-21; 26:9-23), but Paul's own witness to the "newness" that has transformed his life is most impressive.

Primitive Confessions of Faith

We cannot be sure of the details of the instruction that the former zealous Jew received as a new Christian, but Galatians 1:17-18 and Acts 9:19b-30; 11:25-26 indicate that he spent some time away from the missionary activity of the earliest community before he burst upon the scene. In his First Letter to the Corinthians, written in 54 CE, Paul warns his enthusiastic new converts about some of their practices. He tells them what Jesus did at a meal with his disciples on the night before he died, and the events that marked Jesus' resurrection. In both instructions, Paul informs the Corinthians that he is passing on to them what he himself received from those earliest Christians who had instructed him (1 Cor 11:23; 15:3). Paul passes on a *tradition* that is earlier than his conversion, which we can most likely date in early 31 CE, only a year or so after the death of Jesus in 30 CE.

Careful attention to Paul's writing shows that he made his own a number of what we call pre-Pauline expressions of faith. The expression "pre-Pauline" is used to indicate that they go back to the very beginnings of the Christians' attempts to articulate what they believed. A sign of this can be found in the regular use of the expressions "proclaim" … "believe" … "confess" … "that" (Phil 2:11; Rom 10:8b-9; 1 Thess 4:14).

And every tongue should confess that Jesus Christ is Lord (Phil 2:11).

The word of faith which we proclaim; because if you confess with your lips that Jesus is Lord and believe in your heart that God raised him from the dead, you will be saved (Rom 10:8b- 9).

For since we believe that Jesus died and rose again, even so through Jesus, God will bring with him those who have died (1 Thess 4:14).

The affirmation of the death and resurrection of Jesus as constituting his Lordship came to Paul from his earliest days as a Christian. Other pre-Pauline formulae can be sensed behind the following Pauline affirmations, all taken from the Letter to the Romans, Paul's most systematic explanation of his version of the "good news" of what God had done in and through Jesus:

It will be reckoned to us who believe in him who raised Jesus our Lord from the dead, who was handed over to death for our trespasses and was raised for our justification (Rom 4:24-25).

It is Christ Jesus who died, yes, who was raised, who is at the right hand of God (Rom 8:34).

For to this end Christ died and lived again, so that he might be Lord both of the dead and the living (Rom 14:9).

A feature of these selected ancient witnesses is the dominant role of God who raises Jesus from the dead, and God's subsequent establishment of Jesus as Lord. Scholars have identified many such passages (Rom 6:4, 9; 7:4; 8:11; 1 Cor 6:14; 15:15; 2 Cor 4:14; 5:15; 1 Thess 1:10). These earliest passages, which originated in the preaching of the pre-Pauline Church, insist that God intervened into the death of the man called "Jesus" (1 Thess 1:10), and empowered him as "Lord" (1 Cor 6:14), and "Christ" (1 Cor 15:15).

We customarily use the name "Jesus Christ" as if that was Jesus' regular name. Of course it was not, as to call Jesus of Nazareth "the Christ" is to honour him as the Messiah. But for a well-instructed Paul, this honour was taken for granted. He had no hesitation in using "Jesus Christ" as the name for Jesus of Nazareth. Guided by the Spirit, he had been convinced by those who went before him of the truth of "the gospel concerning his Son who was descended from David according to the flesh and was declared to be Son of God with power according to the spirit of holiness by resurrection from the dead, Christ our Lord" (Rom 1:3-4).

1 Corinthians 15:3-8

The pre-Pauline indications of the faith of the earliest Christians, and its proclamation, are brief statements. No doubt there were many such faith-filled exclamations that also formed part of the earliest preaching that have not come down to us in a written form. They impressed Paul so much that he made some of them his own, and he thus preserves for us some of our most ancient confessions of faith in the risen Jesus.

But there is a unique pre-Pauline passage that performs a rare function in Paul's First Letter to the Corinthians: it tells the story of Jesus' death, resurrection, and appearances (1 Cor 15:3-8). Paul rarely indulges in what we call "narrative", or "stories." But in his instruction of the Corinthians who are misunderstanding the meaning of Paul's teaching on resurrection, he begins by reminding them of Jesus' resurrection by telling them a story impregnated with elements from the tradition. The expressions used in the passage continue the style of the earliest confessions.

For I handed on to you as of first importance what I in turn had received (v. 3a):

that Christ died for our sins in accordance with the Scriptures (v.3b),

and that he was buried, and that he was raised on the third day in accordance with the Scriptures (v. 4),

and that he appeared to Cephas, then to the twelve (v. 5).

Then he appeared to more than five hundred brothers and sisters at one time, most of whom are still alive, though some have died (v. 6).

Then he appeared to James, then to all the apostles (v. 7).

Last of all, as to one untimely born, he appeared to me (v. 8).

Paul opens his narrative by insisting upon the fact that what he is passing on to the Corinthians came to him from the earliest Christian tradition. In a parallel use of the story of the Last Supper in 1 Corinthians 11:23-25, he claims that such traditions are "from the Lord" (v. 23). This is a matter "of first importance" (15:3a). He then takes up a pre-Pauline traditional confession of faith. It runs as far as v. 5. It is easily identified by

The use of "raised on the third day" (v. 4) comes from the historical fact that "on the third day" (Friday – Saturday – Sunday) an empty tomb was found, and witnesses encountered the risen Lord. From this initial historical experience the "third day" expression entered into Christian language and literature.

The "story" told in vv. 3b-5 reaches back to the first weeks and months after the death of Jesus. Even at that early stage, it is clear that the Christians were not primarily interested in the facts of the death, the burial, the resurrection, and the appearances. Jesus' death was "for our sins", and "in accordance with the scriptures" (v. 3b). His being raised was "in accordance with the scriptures" (v. 4b). It took place "on the third day" (v. 4). His appearances were experiences that gave birth to faith in Jesus as the founding figure of the Christian community (v. 5). On that basis, Paul can continue the story, indicating the origins of those who have received authority as witnesses (v. 6) and apostles (vv. 7-8).

the rhythmic use of the word "that", so important in confessions of faith, followed by what is confessed:

+ *that* Christ died (v. 3b)
+ *that* he was buried (v. 4a)
+ *that* he was raised (v. 4b)
+ *that* he appeared (v. 5)

The remaining verses in the narrative (vv. 6-8) tell of the appearances of the Risen Jesus to a large group of Christian brethren, James, the apostles, and finally, to Paul. These verses come from Paul's own pen and serve to link the bedrock traditional confessions of vv. 3b-5 to his own mission as an apostle. However, he is bold enough to affirm that there are some still alive who have experienced the risen Lord. If anyone doubts what has been claimed in vv. 3b-5, then they can have first-hand witness from those to whom Jesus appeared who are still alive, even though some are dead (v. 6). They can also find such witness with James, the apostles, and finally, from Paul the apostle (vv. 7-8). He then develops the theme of his apostolic authority in vv. 9-11. Such authority grounds the teaching he will share with the Corinthian community about the *fact* of the resurrection of the dead (vv. 12-34), and the *nature* of risen life (vv. 35-53).

The "story" told in vv. 3b-5 reaches back to the first weeks and months after the death of Jesus. Even at that early stage, it is clear that the Christians were not primarily interested in the facts of the death, the burial, the resurrection, and the appearances. Jesus' death was "for our sins", and "in accordance with the scriptures" (v. 3b). His being raised was "in accordance with the scriptures" (v. 4b). It took place "on the third day" (v. 4). His appearances were experiences that gave birth to

faith in Jesus as the founding figure of the Christian community (v. 5). On that basis, Paul can continue the story, indicating the origins of those who have received authority as witnesses (v. 6) and apostles (vv. 7-8). Much scholarly discussion surrounds the detail of this early confession of 1 Corinthians 15:3b-5. Jesus' death for our sins has its theological roots in the early identification of Jesus' suffering and death with the Suffering Servant of Isaiah (Isa 53:4-6), and the recent Jewish understanding of the deaths of the Maccabean martyrs as "for the people" (2 Macc 7:37-38; 4 Macc 6:27; 17:22; 18:4). The claim that his death (v. 3b) and his resurrection (v. 4) are the fulfilment of scripture has its origins in the life and teaching of Jesus. He looked back to the image of "one like a son of man" in Daniel 7:13-14 and regularly called himself "the Son of Man". Daniel wrote of the suffering and ultimate vindication and victory of God for the holy ones of the most high: the faithful people of Israel. Jesus applied the expression to himself as "the Son of Man", thus using the Prophet Daniel as the "scripture" that pointed forward to his own suffering, forthcoming death, and vindication by God. The earliest tradition saw that this Scripture, used by Jesus himself, had been fulfilled in the death and resurrection of Jesus.

Finally, the use of "raised on the third day" (v. 4) comes from the historical fact that "on the third day" (Friday – Saturday – Sunday) an empty tomb was found, and witnesses encountered the risen Lord. From this initial historical experience the "third day" expression entered into Christian language and literature.

Almost immediately after the earliest Church experienced the risen Jesus, they began to develop an understanding of *what it meant*.

The death of Jesus had, in some way, atoned for sin. The death and resurrection of Jesus were not an "accident". They fulfilled the scriptures, as Jesus had prophesied. In this way his death and resurrection continued God's plan for the perfection of God's loving and saving presence to Israel, and to the whole world. Jesus' appearances did not take place to "prove" anything. They established a divinely instituted authority; God has broken into history, and established a new order. This is what was meant in the early Church when they cried out: "Jesus is Lord!" A new community and a new age began with the presence of the risen Jesus.

Some two thousand years later, believing Christians are able to resonate with these earliest confessions of belief in God's action in and through Jesus, whose loving self-gift in death forgives sin. We continue to experience the Lordship of the risen Christ, as we live in the graced time of the Church, and await the final coming of the Son of Man. Paul developed his splendid

> We customarily use the name "Jesus Christ" as if that was Jesus' regular name. Of course it was not, as to call Jesus of Nazareth "the Christ" is to honour him as the Messiah. But for a well-instructed Paul, this honour was taken for granted. He had no hesitation in using "Jesus Christ" as the name for Jesus of Nazareth.

understanding of the significance of what God has done for us in and through Jesus' death and resurrection on the basis of these truths. Paul rightly understands the bloody event of Jesus' death as the perfect response of obedience to God, reversing the disobedience that marked the beginnings of the biblical story in the Book of Genesis. God's raising Jesus from the dead establishes him as Messiah and Lord. **We live within the graced world of a "new creation" yet still await the final coming of our Messiah and Lord at the end of all time. Both living a Christian life within the community and waiting for the end-time can be called "eschatological". Jesus' death and resurrection generate a "new creation" (Gal 6:15; 2 Cor 5:17) already marked by God's presence as Jesus is *now* our Christ and Lord, but the perfection of all creation in God's definitive Lordship *lies ahead of us* (1 Thess 1:10; Rom 8:18-25).**

SUMMING UP

+ Paul did not create his interpretation of the death and resurrection, but developed it on the basis of the earliest Christians' confessions of faith.

+ These earliest confessions of faith are easily identifiable, reflecting what was originally a spoken proclamation, or an enthusiastic expression of faith.

+ All the earliest witnesses insist upon the action of God, who raised Jesus from the dead, establishing him as Messiah and Lord.

+ One of Paul's very few narratives came to him from pre-Pauline tradition. It is found in 1 Corinthians 15:3-5, expanded by Paul in vv. 7-8, and affirms the basic truths about the resurrection of Jesus.

+ From its earliest times, beginning "on the third day", the members of the Christian community did not overly concern themselves with what happened to Jesus at the resurrection; they sought to explain what it means for humankind.

+ Paul based himself upon earliest Christian faith and developed his foundational and inspired profound Theology and Christology across his Letters.

Chapter Two
The Gospels: Born in the Resurrection

Confessions of faith in God's raising the crucified Jesus to life, and establishing him as Christ and Lord, emerged at the beginning of the Christian community in early 30 CE. Paul developed those confessions into his foundational Theology, Christology, and understanding of the Christian community itself (Ecclesiology) through the Letters that he wrote to various communities in the expanding Church, from 50-60 CE. He was most likely martyred in Rome about 64 CE. No doubt the "story" of the succession of events that marked Jesus' death and resurrection was told and retold as Christians preached a Christ crucified, "a stumbling block to Jews and foolishness to Gentiles" (1 Cor 1:23). There is clear evidence for the very early existence of a basic "passion story" across the Gospels.

Although the accounts of Mark, Matthew, Luke, and especially John, differ in many ways, once they come to tell of the end of Jesus' life, they all have the same sequence of events: final evening with the disciples, arrest in Gethsemane, Jewish hearing, Roman hearing, crucifixion, burial, the discovery of an empty tomb, appearances (not in Mark).

> All four Gospels depend upon a very early "passion story" that existed before Mark wrote, but the authors tell *the same story in different ways*. They do this because, like all early Christians, they were not primarily interested in *what happened to Jesus* at the resurrection, but in *what the resurrection means to believers*.

But the first *written* account of the life, teaching, death, and resurrection of Jesus does not appear until about 70 CE: the Gospel of Mark. The "stories" that conclude all four Gospels began to appear in a written form 40 years after Jesus' crucifixion. The Gospel of John, the last inspired account to appear, was written 70 years after the events it describes.

All four Gospels depend upon a very early "passion story" that existed before Mark wrote, but the authors tell the same story in different ways. They do this because, like all early Christians, they were not primarily interested in what happened to Jesus at the resurrection, but in what the resurrection means to believers.

While Mark, Matthew, Luke, and John certainly looked back to the events that marked Jesus' end, they were more concerned to look to the

communities for whom they were writing their Gospels, and beyond those communities into the larger world of the emerging Christian Church.

Before we begin our journey through the accounts of the resurrection of Jesus, and their significance for a Christian understanding of the resurrection of Jesus and its significance, we need to establish some basic facts about the Gospels, their relationship, and the traditions they received and passed on. Although later than Paul, they also can claim to be repeating Paul's task with the Corinthians: "I handed on to you as of first importance what I in turn had received: that Christ died for our sins in accordance with the scriptures, and that he was buried and that he was raised on the third day in accordance with the scriptures, and that he appeared" (1 Cor 15:3b-5a).

Mark, writing in 70 CE, was the first to look back to that basic tradition, and to the "passion story" that was being told and retold among the Christians, to construct his resurrection account (Mark 16:1-8). As the first written story of Jesus, Mark's Gospel is a remarkable and historical literary event. Mark tells the story of Jesus so that his future audience will remain firm in their belief that, despite rejection, suffering, and death, Jesus of Nazareth is the Christ, the Son of God (Mark 1:1; 14:62; 15:39). Most likely, his focus upon Jesus' suffering and his invitation to all who wish to follow him to take up their cross (8:34) is motivated by the fact that his first audience was experiencing fear, failure, suffering, and death at the hands of the Romans.

The Gospels of Matthew and Luke were written some 15 to 20 years later, but *both Matthew and Luke are aware of Mark's original account.* Indeed, Matthew follows Mark quite closely in some passages, but uses his own traditions in others, as we will see.

Matthew wished to affirm a Jewish-Christian Church of their ongoing relationship to the God of Israel. They were his people, even though they confessed faith in Jesus and had broken with traditional Judaism (Matt 28:16-20).

Luke is more creative. We will sense echoes of Mark's account, but Luke is more original and has significant traditions of his own. He reaches out to Christian Churches in a Gentile world, the results of a Gentile mission, assuring them that they are the result of a long journey that had its beginning in Jesus, but which must journey on, as the risen Jesus travels with them (Luke 24: 13-35).

John is different again, and there is little evidence for any literary dependence upon Mark. His focus is upon a variety of faith experiences of the foundational disciples (Peter, Mary Magdalene, the disciples, and Thomas). He writes at the end of the first Christian century, telling an audience that had never "seen" Jesus that they are especially blessed (John 20:29). His book is written so that, even without experience of the physical Jesus (like the Beloved Disciple [20:8]), they may believe that he is the Christ, the Son of God, and that they may have life in his name (20:29-31).

Despite these different nuances in the four Gospel stories of the resurrection, they are all based upon a primitive resurrection tradition.

The elements of that tradition are:
✟ The discovery of an empty tomb by women (Mark 16:1-2; Matt 28:1; Luke 24:1-3; John 20:1-2). In the Gospel of John there is only one woman, Mary Magdalene.

Matthew 28:1-7
The Resurrection of Jesus

28 After the sabbath, as the first day of the week was dawning, Mary Magdalene and the other Mary went to see the tomb. 2 And suddenly there was a great earthquake; for an angel of the Lord, descending from heaven, came and rolled back the stone and sat on it. 3 His appearance was like lightning, and his clothing white as snow. 4 For fear of him the guards shook and became like dead men. 5 But the angel said to the women, "Do not be afraid; I know that you are looking for Jesus who was crucified. 6 He is not here; for he has been raised, as he said. Come, see the place where he[a] lay. 7 Then go quickly and tell his disciples, 'He has been raised from the dead,[b] and indeed he is going ahead of you to Galilee; there you will see him.' This is my message for you."

- The presence of interpreting figures (men or angels) at the tomb (Mark 16:3-5; Matt 28:2-4; Luke 24:4; John 20:12-13).

- An Easter proclamation that Jesus has been raised (Mark 16:5-6; Matt 28:5-6; Luke 24:5-6; John 20:17-18).

- Appearances (except in Mark's original ending [see below]) (Matt 28:9, 16-20; Luke 24:13-35, 36-50; John 20:11-17, 19-23, 26-29; 21:1-23).

- A commission (Mark 16:7; Matt 28:17-20; Luke 24:46-49; John 20:21-23).

As we will see, these solid building blocks of the primitive resurrection tradition will be developed and told in different ways by each Evangelist. The authors are certainly imaginative, and they are also depending upon independent older traditions, for example, Luke's account of the journey to Emmaus (Luke 24:13-35).

But Mark, Matthew, Luke, and John share and proclaim their belief in the discovery of an empty tomb, God's action that rendered Jesus alive among them, and the concern for the ongoing mission of the Church.

> Matthew wished to affirm a Jewish-Christian Church of their ongoing relationship to the God of Israel. They were his people, even though they confessed faith in Jesus, and had broken with traditional Judaism (Matt 28:16-20).

Two further clarifications are called for before we turn our attention to each of the Gospel stories. In your printed editions of the New Testament, the Gospel of Mark ends with Mark 16:1-20. However, you will notice that all editions indicate that vv. 9-20 were added by scribes, most likely late in the second Christian century. As Mark 16:8 ends with the words "they said nothing to anyone for they were afraid," later scribes added the present vv.9-20 to provide a more satisfactory ending, more in keeping with the other Gospels. The original Gospel ended with v. 8, and our reflection on Mark's resurrection message is based on those eight brief verses.

You will also notice that John's Gospel appears to close in John 20:30-31. However, without any explanation, another resurrection chapter, featuring a further appearance of the risen Jesus, follows (21:1-25). Our reflection must attend to John 21, as there has never been a copy of the Gospel of John, from our earliest manuscripts, without that chapter. Unlike Mark 16:9-20, which was added to the oldest scripts of the Gospel by later scribes, John 21:1-25 is found in our earliest manuscripts. We will see that it is a "necessary epilogue," and not a mere addition ("addendum") to the Gospel.

SUMMING UP

- Jesus' death by crucifixion was the most serious problem that the earliest Church had to face in its preaching.

- Paul's teaching did not shy clear of that truth, but made it the centre-piece of his teaching.

- The earliest Church also "told the story" of Jesus' passion, death and resurrection. The earliest written account that we have is in the Gospel of Mark.

- All four Gospels are based upon the same traditions, but shape their telling of the story to address the needs and questions of their audiences.

- Mark 16:9-20 does not belong to the Gospel of Mark, while John 21:1-25 does belong to the Gospel of John.

Chapter Three: The Gospel of Mark

Mark 16:1-8
The Resurrection of Jesus

16 When the sabbath was over, Mary Magdalene, and Mary the mother of James, and Salome bought spices, so that they might go and anoint him. 2 And very early on the first day of the week, when the sun had risen, they went to the tomb. 3 They had been saying to one another, "Who will roll away the stone for us from the entrance to the tomb?" 4 When they looked up, they saw that the stone, which was very large, had already been rolled back. 5 As they entered the tomb, they saw a young man, dressed in a white robe, sitting on the right side; and they were alarmed. 6 But he said to them, "Do not be alarmed; you are looking for Jesus of Nazareth, who was crucified. He has been raised; he is not here. Look, there is the place they laid him. 7 But go, tell his disciples and Peter that he is going ahead of you to Galilee; there you will see him, just as he told you." 8 So they went out and fled from the tomb, for terror and amazement had seized them; and they said nothing to anyone, for they were afraid.[a]

Mark opens his resurrection story with the words: "And when the Sabbath was passed" (16:1). He continues his account of the burial of Jesus that ended: "t was the day of Preparation, that is, the day before the Sabbath". The women of 16:1b (Mary Magdalene, Mary the mother of James and Joses, and Salome) are the same ones who watched the death of Jesus from afar (15:40). Two of them (Mary Magdalene and Mary the mother of Joses) had also seen where the body of Jesus was laid (15:47).

The account has three moments:
✠ Women at the Tomb (vv. 1-4).

✠ The Easter Proclamation (vv. 5-7).

✠ The Failure of the Women (v. 8).

Women at the Tomb (vv. 1-4)

The women brought spices so that they might go and anoint Jesus' body. Joseph of Arimathea had buried Jesus without the usual washing and anointing of the body in 15:46. The women come to the tomb to render respect to the person whom they have seen slain (15:40-41) and buried (15:47). They are not prepared for what they discover. They proceed to the site of the tomb "very early on the first day of the week" (v. 2). It is the "third day", and the audience recalls that Jesus spoke of his being raised on that day (8:31; 9:31; 10:34; 14:58; 15:29). The time of the day is "when the sun had risen" (v. 2). The rising of the sun is a first indication to the audience that the darkness that enveloped the earth as the agonising Son asked his Father why he had abandoned him (15:33-37) has been overcome. Light is dawning as God enters the story, but the women are not aware of that truth. They ask one another who will roll away the stone covering the opening into the tomb (v. 3; 15:46). If three women would not be able to roll back the stone, it must have been very large.

God's action has already overcome the women's difficulty.

Raising their eyes, they saw that the stone had been rolled back (v. 4a). The passive form of a past tense of the verb invites the audience to ask who rolled back the stone, "which was very large" (v. 4b, v. 3). God has entered the story. Grammarians call this use of the verb the "divine passive". There is no one else who could have rolled back the stone except God, to whom Jesus cried out in anguish in his dying moments (15:34).

Mark uses two verbs: the women *raised* their eyes and they *saw* (16:4a). This is a solemn moment, and no ordinary seeing. The women see what God has already done. The most important character has entered the narrative: God has overcome the darkness and has opened the seemingly impossible to open (vv. 2-4).

Easter Proclamation (vv. 5-7)

On penetrating the tomb, the women see a young man seated on the right side of the tomb, dressed in a white robe. The response of the women is extreme amazement. The original Greek means that the women were "amazed out of themselves". Their shocked reaction matches traditional biblical responses to the appearance of the divine. The presence of the young man on the right side of the tomb announces that the tomb is empty, before even a word is spoken. They do not find the body of Jesus, but a young man.

He is a messenger from God, but the audience recalls the earlier reference to the "young man" in 14:51-52. He was a symbol of the failed disciples who fled in fear, naked in their nothingness as they separated themselves from Jesus when he was arrested. Unable to deny themselves, take up the cross and follow him (8:34), despite their protestations that they would die for him (14:31), in fear they abandon Jesus to his death. The young man in the parable on the disciples left "a linen cloth" in the hands of Jesus' assailants when he ran away in fear (14:52). The young man in the tomb is dressed in "a white robe" (16:5). But the body of Jesus was wrapped in "a linen cloth" (15:46). There is no sign in the tomb of this garment of death. The young man in the garden was "clothed"(14:51) but ran away "naked" (14:52). The young man in the tomb is "clothed", and the verb used for "clothed" in 14:51 returns in 16:5.

The young man who fled naked in 14:51-52, has not been dismissed from the story. Dressed in a white robe, he announces what God has done to the one who had been laid in the tomb (v. 6). As God has transformed the death of Jesus by raising him from the dead, discipleship will be re-established and nakedness covered (14:51-52). God's action can reverse failure. As God has done with the apparent failure of the crucified Jesus, so can he do for the disciples who have fled in fear (14:51-52). They betrayed their Master (14:10-11, 43-46), and denied him (14:53, 66-72).

The young man, as in all biblical divine appearances, urges the women not to be afraid (v. 6a). He first describes what the woman have experienced: "You are seeking Jesus, the Nazarene, who was crucified" (16:6a). They are asked to look again at the place where he was laid: 'He is not here" (v. 6c). The young man explains why: "He has been raised!" (v. 6b). Another divine passive is used

(v. 4). A past tense and the passive form of the verb indicate that God had already entered the story of Jesus before the women appeared on the scene. Human experience and expectation have been transcended by the action of God.

The question asked of God by Jesus from the cross, "My God, my God, why have you forsaken me?" (15:34) has been answered. Jesus has not been forsaken. Unconditionally obedient to the will of God (14:36), Jesus has accepted the cup of suffering. On the cross he is Messiah, King of Israel and Son of God (14:62; 15:32, 39). God's never-failing presence to his obedient Son leads to the definitive action of God: he has been raised! The opponents of Jesus crucified him, and they placed his body in a tomb ("look at the place where *they* laid him"). It could appear that they had their victory, but they have been thwarted. Jesus the Nazarene has been raised by God.

During the life and ministry of Jesus, the disciples were commissioned to establish a new family of God (3:13-19, 31-35; 6:7-13) and told that before the end of time the Gospel would be preached to all nations (13:10). They have disappeared from the story, fleeing in fear, naked in their nothingness (14:50-52). The young man commissions the women to announce a message to the failed disciples. The promise of the restoration of these disciples was first made by Jesus to his disciples as they walked away from their last meal: "After I am raised up, I *will go* [future tense] before you into Galilee" (14:28). The future tense of 14:28 is now rendered as a present tense in the young man's instruction to the women: "But go, tell his disciples and Peter that he *is going* [present tense] before you into Galilee, as he told you" (v. 7). Jesus' ministry began in Galilee (1:14-15). He called the disciples, and they began their mission in Galilee (2:13-14; 3:13-14; 6:6b-30). They are to return to the place of their enthusiastic beginnings and resume their mission in the place that the Prophet Isaiah called "Galilee of the Gentiles" (Isaiah 9:1).

In 10:32 the reader learnt that the disciples were on the way toward Jerusalem because Jesus "was going before them", leading them to Jerusalem, the place of his passion, death and resurrection. His promise, that he would later lead them away from the city of their fear and failure so that they might see him in Galilee (14:28), will be fulfilled (16:7). Despite their fear (4:40; 6:50; 9:32; 10:32), failure (e.g. 4:35-41; 6:35-36; 8:4, 31-33; 9:32-34; 10:35-41; 11:9-10), and flight (14:50), he is again "going before them" back to Galilee. They will see him there, as he had promised (16:7; 14:28).

Failure (v. 8)

This promise appears to be thwarted by the last line of the Gospel: "And

> Raising their eyes they saw that the stone *had been rolled back* (v. 4a). The passive form of a past tense of the verb invites the audience to ask who rolled back the stone, "which was very large" (v. 4b, v. 3). God has entered the story. Grammarians call this use of the verb the "divine passive". There is no one else who could have rolled back the stone except God, to whom Jesus cried out in anguish in his dying moments (15:34).

> The women, who had overcome the scandal of the cross by looking on from afar as Jesus died (15:40-41), and had watched where he was buried (15:47), are overcome by an empty tomb and the Easter proclamation. They have joined the disciples in flight (14:50, 52) and fear (4:41, 6:50, 9:32, 10:32). The women's sharing of the fear and flight of the disciples must be given its full importance, properly to understand Mark's Easter message.

they went out and fled from the tomb; for trembling and astonishment had come upon them; and they said nothing to anyone, for they were afraid" (v. 8).

The women, who had overcome the scandal of the cross by looking on from afar as Jesus died (15:40-41), and had watched where he was buried (15:47), are overcome by an empty tomb and the Easter proclamation. They have joined the disciples in flight (14:50, 52) and fear (4:41; 6:50; 9:32; 10:32). The women's sharing of the fear and flight of the disciples must be given its full importance, to properly understand Mark's Easter message.

The disciples had steadily increased in their experience of fear across the story (4:41; 5:36; 6:50; 9:32; 10:32). They finally broke their oneness with him when they fled (14:50; 3:14). The women share in one of the fundamental aspects of the disciples' failure to follow Jesus to the cross: fear (4:41; 6:50; 9:32; 10:32). Mark 16:1-8 is the masterstroke of a story-teller who, up to this point, has relentlessly pursued the steady movement to failure of all the male disciples. He now adds the failure of the women, who until now have been so valiant. But Matthew 28:1-10, Luke 24:1-12, and John 20:1-3, 17-18 indicate that women were the first witnesses of the Easter event to unbelieving and discouraged disciples. As we have seen, the even earlier evidence of 1 Corinthians 15:5 confesses that the risen Jesus appeared to "Cephas and the twelve." *But Mark has changed the ending.*

Promises fulfilled

As with the prophecies of Jesus' forthcoming death and resurrection (8:31; 9:31; 10:33-34), the promises of 14:28 and 16:7 will be fulfilled. *What Jesus said would happen, will happen.* His betrayal, arrest, trials, and crucifixion show that Jesus' predictions come true. Although a meeting with the risen Jesus is not found *in the story*, the *very existence of the story* tells Christian audiences that *what Jesus said would happen, did happen*. The Gospel of Mark addresses a believing community. The young man repeats the promise of Jesus, first made in 14:28: the disciples and Peter "will see" the risen Jesus in Galilee (16:7; 1 Cor 15:5). The disciples and Peter did see Jesus in Galilee, as he had promised (14:28, 16:7), as Jesus' prophecies always come true (8:31; 9:31; 10:32-34, 12:11-12; 14:17-21, 27-31).

There is no record of an encounter with Jesus *in the story*. But if the promise of 14:28 and 16:7 had been thwarted, there would be no Gospel of Mark. The end of Mark's story is the beginning of Christian discipleship, both male and female, restored and empowered in its fear by the action of God, in and through the risen Christ.

SUMMING UP

✙ Mark 16:1-8 is the original end of the Gospel of Mark, despite the strange response of the women in v. 8.

✙ This passage is the oldest narrative of a visit to an empty tomb, the Easter proclamation, and a commission. Matthew and Luke depend upon this original story. John has different sources.

✙ There is a close link between the "young man" of 14:50-52 and the "young man" in the empty tomb in 16:5.

✙ The restoration of discipleship is symbolised by the "young man", and the commission to the women.

✙ The failure of the women is explained by the eventual victory of God, evident in the existence of a Christian community that produced and received the Gospel of Mark.

Chapter Four
The Gospel of Matthew

Matthew 28:16-20
The Commissioning of the Disciples

16 Now the eleven disciples went to Galilee, to the mountain to which Jesus had directed them. 17 When they saw him, they worshiped him; but some doubted. 18 And Jesus came and said to them, "All authority in heaven and on earth has been given to me. 19 Go therefore and make disciples of all nations, baptizing them in the name of the Father and of the Son and of the Holy Spirit, 20 and teaching them to obey everything that I have commanded you. And remember, I am with you always, to the end of the age."[a]

Matthew 28:1-10 has many contacts with Mark 16:1-8. However, once the account of the women at the tomb is reported, he closes his Gospel story in a different fashion.

✚ The women at the tomb and their commission to announce Jesus' resurrection (vv. 1-10).

✚ The guard's report to the Jewish authorities generates bribery and lies (vv. 11-15).

✚ Jesus' appearance to the Eleven and their final commission on a mountain (vv. 16-20).

Women at the Tomb (vv. 1-10)

Matthew states that what follows took place "after the Sabbath … as the first day of the week was breaking", but he changes the names of the women making the journey to the tomb to "Mary Magdalene and the other Mary" (v. 1). These were the women who saw where Jesus was buried (Matt 27:61). There is no reference to anointing. The dawning of a new day signals a new period of history. What follows is only found in Matthew. He describes the events of that moment with language used by Jewish authors to speak of the end-time.

> And suddenly there was a great earthquake; for an angel of the Lord, descending from heaven, came and rolled back the stone and sat on it. His appearance was like lightning, and his clothing white as snow. For fear of him the guards shook and became like dead men (vv. 2-4).

The audience recalls that the death of Jesus was also marked by language associated with the end of the ages (27:45, 51-53).

As at the cross (27:51), an earthquake takes place (Hag 2:6; Zech 14:5), an angel of the Lord with an appearance like lightning descends from heaven (1 Enoch 1:3-9; 20:17-19), and trembling and fear possess the guards (Dan 10:7-9, 16; 12:2). By using descriptions regularly used to mark the end of time, Matthew points to the death and resurrection of Jesus as the turning point of the ages.

The audience recalls words of Jesus as he opened his ministry: The law and the prophets must stand, until heaven and earth pass away (5:18a); everything is now accomplished (5:18b). Heaven and earth are passing away.

Describing Jesus' death (27:51-54) and resurrection (28:2-4) as events marked by the signs of the end time, Matthew teaches that God has anticipated his coming in Jesus' death and resurrection. Jesus of Nazareth is the Emmanuel, God with us (1:23). Time, human history and the ups and downs of human experience

> As at the cross (27:51), an earthquake takes place (Hag 2:6; Zech 14:5), an angel of the Lord with an appearance like lightning descends from heaven (1 Enoch 1:3-9; 20:17-19), and trembling and fear possess the guards (Dan 10:7-9, 16; 12:2). By using descriptions regularly used to mark the end of time, Matthew points to the death and resurrection of Jesus as the turning point of the ages.

will continue, but — for Matthew— everything has been transformed by Jesus' death and resurrection.

Jesus earlier instructed his disciples to observe the Law (5:17-20) and to limit their mission to Israel (10:5-6). Now another time is at hand, as the crucified and risen Jesus sends out his disciples to all nations (28:16-20). One era has come to an end; another is dawning.

Matthew returns to Mark in vv. 5-8 (Mark 16:6-7). The women are told not to fear. The angel who had rolled back the stone knows that they seek Jesus of Nazareth, the crucified one. The women knew Jesus of Nazareth, and they have seen him crucified (27:55-56). The Easter proclamation follows: he is no longer in the tomb. He has been raised, as he said he would. The women are to look at the place where those who killed him allowed him to be buried. They are commissioned to go quickly to the disciples and announce that he has been raised from the dead and is going ahead of them to Galilee (v. 7). The angel takes on the authority of Jesus, instructing them to go into Galilee. It is his word that sends them on their way to Galilee (v. 7). They depart from the tomb "with fear" (Mark 16:8), but they do not flee. Full of great joy, they run to tell the disciples. They are the first to announce the Easter message (Matt 28:8).

A further Matthean addition to Mark 16:1-8 closes the episode of the women at the tomb. On their way to announce the message to the disciples, the risen Jesus met the women, greeting them with a salutation that catches the "great joy" that marked their departure from the tomb: "Rejoice." Their response is a respectful "going to him". Matthew reports the women's approach to Jesus: they approach Jesus, take hold of his feet, and humbly bow before him. The verb used for "bowing down" is one of Matthew's favourite words for the recognition of the presence of the divine in Jesus' story (2:2, 8, 11; 4:9, 10; 8:2; 9:18; 14:33; 15:25; 20:20; 28:17). Jesus sends them on their mission to announce the Easter message to the disciples (Matt 27:10). His command is almost identical to that of the angel in v. 7. However, he does not send them to "the disciples and Peter" (Mark 16:7), but to "my brethren" (v. 10). As the death and resurrection of Jesus marked the turning point of the ages, the recipients of the Easter message are no longer "disciples" but Jesus' brothers and sisters.

Matthew's passion narrative closes with the placing of guards to avoid all possible fraudulent preaching about the risen Jesus (27:62-66). The story has moved from that *negative* response to the cross to the *positive* experience of 28:1-10. The rest of Matthew's resurrection story is found only in Matthew.

The Guard's Report (28:11-15)

A further *negative* scene follows, with its crucial explanation in v. 15. As the women are on their way to announce the resurrection to the disciples, some of the guards from 27:62-66 are simultaneously on their way to the chief priests. Like the women, they also tell "all that had taken place" (v. 11). The two reports, one a lie (vv. 13-14) and the other the truth (vv. 7-8), produce different fruits. The solemn meeting between the guards and the chief priests leads to the decision that the Jewish leaders will bribe the soldiers with money (v. 12). As Judas was led astray with the promise of money (26:14-16), so are the soldiers. They are instructed to tell a lie: "his disciples came by night and stole him away while we were asleep" (v. 13). The leaders are willing to indulge in further dishonesty if any of this comes to the Roman authority (the governor). They will also keep him happy (v. 14).

Matthew concludes: "This story is still told among the Jews to this day" (v. 15). The Matthean community tells the story of the resurrection of Jesus and his appearances; the Jews tell the story of a body stolen by his disciples. The reason for the women's story is their Easter experience of the risen Jesus. The reason for the story told by the Jews is corruption among the leaders of the Jews. For Matthew, Christians are living in the truth of the risen Jesus, while the Jews are living and telling a lie.

Commissioning (28:16-20)

As Jesus opened his ministry with a sermon on a mountain, he taught that every detail of the Law and the Prophets must be taught and observed (5:17-20). Matthew 28:16-20 takes the audience into a new time that lies outside the story of the Gospel, into "the time of the Church" (Matt 16:18; 18:17). Matthew 28:16-20 must be understood against the background that produced this Gospel. It was proclaimed in a time when two religions, once identified as one religion, were searching for their identity. On the one hand, the Matthean Christians were told a story affirming that Jesus is the perfection of all righteousness, the one who generates the true Israel, bringing in a new era in his death and resurrection. On the other hand, post-war Judaism (post 70 CE) attached itself closer to the observance of Torah and its ordinances, finding there a path of truth and life. In Matthew 28:16-20 the community is instructed to move away from Judaism, within which it was born, into a mission to all nations.

Eleven disciples (as Judas has left the Twelve in despair [27:3-10]) went into Galilee, to the mountain, to meet Jesus (v. 16). The reaction of the disciples to the sight of Jesus is ambiguous. Some worship him.

Jesus does not "replace" the Torah, but he "perfects" it (5:17-18). The disciples are not to teach and observe the teaching of the Torah, but the teaching of Jesus. From this point on, the Law will be interpreted through the teaching of Jesus. But there is more to this final command. Jesus' final words are not words of departure, but words assuring that he will always be with his disciples (v. 20b). These words link the end of the Gospel to its beginning. In the annunciation of the birth of Jesus to Joseph in 1:23, Jesus was promised as the Emmanuel, "God with us".

But "some doubted" (v. 17). The hesitation of the disciples in the presence of the risen Lord is one of the hallmarks of the resurrection accounts (Mark 16:8; Luke 24:10-11, 13-35, 36-37; John 20:11-17; 24-29). Resurrection faith can always be touched by unfaith, because God has done the impossible.

Jesus opens his final instructions with a declaration about himself (v. 18). He then spells out the consequences of such a declaration for his disciples and their mission (vv. 19-20). The man whom they had known as Jesus of Nazareth claims that all authority in heaven and on earth has been given to him (v. 18). The risen Jesus has taken over the authority and dignity that traditional Israel allowed only to God (Deut 6:4-9; Dan 7:14). Only on the basis of his claims in v. 18 can Jesus issue the commands that follow: The disciples are to "Go therefore and make disciples of all nations" (v. 19a). They are to make "disciples". The eleven are "disciples," and have been learning from Jesus to this point. Something astonishingly new is commanded by Jesus. There is only one people of God, with its father Abraham and its Law from Moses, the nation Israel. This is reversed: the disciples, a new people of God, founded by Jesus of Nazareth, are to "go out" to make disciples *of all nations*.

They are to "baptize" in the name of the Father and of the Son and of the Holy Spirit (v. 19b). The Christian missionary is told to replace the initiation of circumcision with Baptism. Baptism in the name of the Father, the Son and the Holy Spirit anticipates, but does not teach, the doctrine of the Trinity, which came much later (at the Council of Nicaea in 325 CE). In Jesus' baptism the voice of the Father comes from heaven and the Spirit of God

> There will be a mixture of good and bad within the Church (13:24-30). Many will grow weary waiting for his return (25:1-13), but at the end of the age Jesus will come as the Son of Man to judge the nations (25:31-46).
> Thus the great commission (28:16-20) is not an ending but a beginning that invites the audience to discipleship and to the evangelization of the nations in the period between the death and resurrection of Jesus and the final coming of the Son of Man.

And suddenly there was a great earthquake; for an angel of the Lord, descending from heaven, came and rolled back the stone and sat on it. His appearance was like lightning, and his clothing white as snow. For fear of him the guards shook and became like dead men (vv. 2-4).

descends upon Jesus (3:16-17). The Baptism practiced in the Matthean Church must have used a formula over the newly baptised that is recorded here: Father, Son, and Holy Spirit.

Jesus does not "replace" the Torah, but he "perfects" it (5:17-18). The disciples are not to teach and observe the teaching of the Torah, but the teaching of Jesus. From this point on, the Law will be interpreted through the teaching of Jesus. But there is more to this final command. Jesus' final words are not words of departure, but words assuring that he will always be with his disciples (v. 20b). These words link the end of the Gospel to its beginning. In the annunciation of the birth of Jesus to Joseph in 1:23, Jesus was promised as the Emmanuel, "God with us". Although the story ends here, the audience is aware that there will be periods of persecution when many will fall away (13:21).

There will be a mixture of good and bad within the Church (13:24-30). Many will grow weary waiting for his return (25:1-13), but at the end of the age Jesus will come as the Son of Man to judge the nations (25:31-46). Thus the great commission (28:16-20) is not an ending but a beginning that invites the audience to discipleship and to the evangelisation of the nations in the period between the death and resurrection of Jesus and the final coming of the Son of Man.

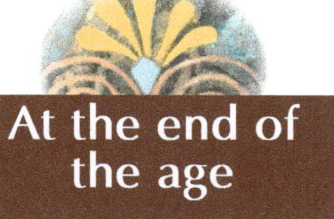

At the end of the age

As the risen Lord to whom all authority on earth and in heaven has been given, Jesus can send his disciples to all nations, teaching what he taught them (28:16-20). The heavens are still above, the earth is still firmly in place under their feet, and the end time still lies somewhere in the unknown future! The crucified and risen Jesus will be with his community until the end of the age (28:20). Sent by the Lord of heaven and earth (28:18), the disciples of Jesus, now his brothers and sisters (v. 10), are to carry out their mission in the in-between-time, until the end of the age (28:19-20).

In his final discourse, on the eve of his death and resurrection (24:1-25:6), Jesus instructed his disciples: "And this gospel of the kingdom will be preached throughout the whole world, as a testimony to all nations; and then the end will come" (24:14). None of this would have been possible if God had not acted decisively among us in the death and resurrection of Jesus.

The Church is part of "the in between time", living and proclaiming the Gospel of Jesus, making disciples of all nations until God's final gift, which will come at the end of the age.

SUMMARY

✢ Matthew's account of the women at the empty tomb is close to Mark's account.

✢ Matthew's main addition to the earlier narrative is a description of what happened at the rolling back of the stone, associated with signs that symbolise the end of the ages.

✢ Only Matthew reports Jesus' meeting with the women at the tomb, affirming that his disciples are now his brothers and sisters.

✢ Only Matthew reports the setting of a guard at the tomb and the subsequent report of the guard to the Jewish leadership.

✢ Jesus' final encounter with his disciples on the mountain is a witness to God's plan for the Christian community in the time between the death and resurrection of Jesus and God's final return.

Chapter Five
The Gospel of Luke

Luke 24:28-35

28 As they came near the village to which they were going, he walked ahead as if he were going on. 29 But they urged him strongly, saying, "Stay with us, because it is almost evening and the day is now nearly over." So he went in to stay with them. 30 When he was at the table with them, he took bread, blessed and broke it, and gave it to them. 31 Then their eyes were opened, and they recognized him; and he vanished from their sight. 32 They said to each other, "Were not our hearts burning within us[a] while he was talking to us on the road, while he was opening the scriptures to us?" 33 That same hour they got up and returned to Jerusalem; and they found the eleven and their companions gathered together. 34 They were saying, "The Lord has risen indeed, and he has appeared to Simon!" 35 Then they told what had happened on the road, and how he had been made known to them in the breaking of the bread.

An author known to us as "Luke" wrote two volumes that form a large part of the New Testament: the Gospel of Luke and the Acts of the Apostles. Sharing meals and "journeys" are important to Luke. In the Gospel, there are 51 references to food and eating. The journey of Jesus to Jerusalem in Luke 9:51-19:44 and the journeys of Paul in Acts 13:1-28:31 from Antioch to Rome dominate the Gospel and Acts. These themes continue into the resurrection account. Jesus shares meals with disciples at Emmaus in Luke 24:23-32 and with all the disciples in vv. 41-43. The "journey" to Emmaus (vv. 13-35) is well-known. Only Luke's account of the women at the tomb (vv. 1-12) comes from the tradition common to Mark and Matthew (Mark 16:1-8; Matt 28:1-10).

All the episodes of Luke's resurrection account took place on the *one day*. The account opens with the naming of a given day: "On the first day of the week" (v. 1). The reader is next told, "Now on that same day two of them were going to a village called Emmaus" (v. 13). Towards the end of their journey, Jesus' fellow-travellers say: "Stay with us, because it is almost evening and the day is nearly over" (v. 29). After the breaking of the bread, "That same hour they got up and returned to Jerusalem." They make their report, but, "While they were talking about this, Jesus himself stood among them" (v. 36). At the end of the day, he leaves them in his ascension into heaven (v. 51).

Luke's Gospel has been directed towards this "day". As Jesus began his journey towards Jerusalem in 9:51, the narrator commented, "When the days drew near for him to be taken up, he set his face to go to Jerusalem." That "journey" ends in Jerusalem. The centre-point of Luke-Acts is the city of Jerusalem. The journey of Jesus leads him there (19:45). In Jerusalem the Paschal events take place (19:45-24:49), and he ascends to his Father from the city (24:50-51). Jerusalem is the end of the journey of Jesus, and the journey of the apostles begins there.

The risen Jesus commissions them to go out to all the nations, but they are to "stay here in the city" to await the gift of the Spirit (24:49). There they are given the Spirit (Acts 2:1-13). There they first become "church", one in heart and soul, celebrating the Lord's presence in their meals (Acts 2:42-47) just as they celebrated with Jesus throughout his

> Luke's resurrection account is focused upon the city of Jerusalem and the "day".

ministry, and especially with the risen Jesus (Luke 24:13-35, 36-48). They eventually set out from Jerusalem, witnesses "in Judea and Samaria and to the ends of the earth" (Acts 1:8; 20:7-11; 27:33-36). The city of Jerusalem and the events of that "day" of the resurrection act as a fulcrum, around which God's saving history swivels.

Luke's resurrection account is focused upon the city of Jerusalem and the "day".

✦ Women find an empty tomb in Jerusalem (vv. 1-12).

✦ The journey to Emmaus and the return to Jerusalem (vv. 13-35).

✦ The risen Jesus shares a meal, instructs and commissions his disciples in Jerusalem, where they are to stay until they are given the gift of the Spirit (vv. 36-49).

✦ The ascension of Jesus from Jerusalem (vv. 50-56).

However much the story that Luke tells has been shaped by the tradition that came to him, Luke exercises great originality and reports otherwise unheard-of events.

Women at the Tomb (vv. 1-12)

Luke smooths out the names of the women who are at the cross, see the burial place, and visit the tomb. He also recalls his earlier information that these women had come with Jesus from Galilee, those who "followed" Jesus to his burial in 23:55-56 (8:1-3). They have seen to the preparation of the spices in the interval between the burial of Jesus and "the first day of the week" (23:56a; 24:1). The discovery of the empty tomb (vv. 2-3) leaves them perplexed, not overwhelmed or amazed (v. 4a; Mark 16:4-5). In their perplexity, they are confronted with two men, dressed in dazzling apparel (v. 4b). The women, who bow their faces to the ground in a gesture of reverence and unworthiness, recognise that these figures are heavenly messengers (v. 5a).

The two men ask why the women are seeking Jesus in a cemetery. If they wish to find Jesus, they will not find him among the dead because: "He is not here, but has been raised" (v. 6a. AT). The risen Jesus will not be found in a cemetery!

The men ask them to "remember" Jesus' word to them (v. 6b). They are to recall the message of Jesus from their time with him in Galilee (8:1-3). The women have journeyed with Jesus from Galilee to Jerusalem. During the journey they have heard Jesus speak of his forthcoming death and resurrection on three occasions (9:22, 44; 18:31-33). What Jesus had promised has taken place. He was delivered into the hands of sinful people, and they crucified him. It is now the third day since he was slain, and the final part of Jesus' prophecy was: "and on the third day rise" (v. 7; 9:22).

Shortly, soon after his first prophecy of his passion and resurrection in 9:22, Jesus repeats it, along with an instruction: "Let these words sink into your ears" (9:44). The women's search for Jesus in a graveyard indicates that his earlier words to them are unheeded. Thus they are commanded: "Remember!" (v. 6).

And they "remembered his words" (v. 8), leave the place of the dead (v. 9a), and announce the Easter message to the disciples (v. 9b). Unlike Mark (16:7) and Matthew (28:7), the women are not asked to tell the disciples that the risen Jesus is going ahead of them into Galilee. For Luke, all the saving events surrounding Jesus' passion, death and resurrection take place in Jerusalem. The Galilee tradition is not forgotten, as the women must remember what Jesus told them in Galilee (v. 6a). In v. 10 the women who had travelled with Jesus from Galilee (8:1-3) and had further followed him to his place of burial (23:55-56) are named: "Mary Magdalene, Joanna, Mary the mother of James and the other women with them." They announce to the disciples that Jesus' promises of 9:22 and 9:44 have come true (v. 10). The group that receives the message of the resurrection is larger than "the disciples and Peter" (Mark 16:7), but they all regard such news as an idle tale (v. 11). This response is a negative evaluation of women, so contrary to Jesus' attitude to women throughout the Gospel of Luke. Nevertheless, Peter "got up and ran to the tomb." There he finds an empty tomb, with the linen burial cloths empty. He wonders what all this might mean.

As with the women (v. 4), so also with Peter (v. 12). His visit to the graveyard allows him to see what the women saw: an empty tomb, and the signs of what the Christian reader can recognise as God's victory over death. But an empty tomb only generates

> The two men ask why the women are seeking Jesus in a cemetery. If they wish to find Jesus, they will not find him among the dead because: "He is not here, but has been raised" (v. 6a. AT). The risen Jesus will not be found in a cemetery!

wonder about what it might mean. Easter faith is not born in a cemetery (vv. 3, 5, 12), but in remembering the words of Jesus (vv. 6-10).

The Journey to Emmaus (vv. 13-35)

The opening remarks of the journey to Emmaus are an indication of the wrong choice made by two disciples. "Now on that same day" two disciples were going to Emmaus, "about sixty stadia away from Jerusalem" (24:13). They are walking *away from Jerusalem*, the central point of God's sacred history, in disappointment and failure. The paschal events are in the forefront of the disciples' minds, and the subject of their conversation, as they walk away (v. 14) and as the risen Jesus "went with them" (v. 15).

Throughout the Gospel, and spectacularly on the cross, Jesus has reached out to sinners with pardon (23:34) and offered salvation (vv. 39-43). Now, as the risen one, he "walks with" disciples who are abandoning God's saving story.

Luke reports that "their eyes were kept from recognizing him" (v. 16). There is a mysterious "other" directing the presence of Jesus. God is responsible and is not abandoning the failing disciples. Jesus opens the conversation by asking them what they were discussing with one another as they walked. At this question, they stop (v. 17).

Cleopas wonders how this person could even ask such a question. Surely, every visitor to Jerusalem would know "the things that have taken place there in these days" (v. 18). Jesus is indeed a visitor to Jerusalem. Since 9:51, he has journeyed from Galilee to the city. Jesus, who has been at the centre of the events, is also the bearer of their significance. But the two disciples know only of the "events", not their ultimate significance. In response to Jesus' further query, they show their understanding of "what has taken place" in Jerusalem: "We had hoped that he was the one to redeem Israel" (v. 21). They have not yet understood that the resurrection of Jesus is the resurrection of "the Messiah *of God*" (9:20). He is not the Messiah of their expectations.

They know all the events:
✚ Jesus of Nazareth, a prophet mighty in word and deed (v. 19).

✚ "Our chief priests and leaders handed him over to be condemned to death and crucified him" (v. 20).

✚ "It is now the third day" (v. 21); women have been at the tomb early in the morning, but "they did not find his body" (vv. 22-23).

✚ There has been a vision of angels who said: "He is alive!" (v. 23).

✚ Peter has been to the empty tomb: "But they did not see him" (v. 24).

Unlike the women, they have not remembered the words of Jesus (v. 8). They do not understand the *significance* of these *events*. They continue their walk away from Jerusalem.

A liturgy of the Word follows. Jesus chides them for their foolishness and opens "all the scriptures" for them: it was necessary that the Christ should suffer many things to enter his glory (vv. 25-26). Jesus calls to their memory the necessity for the Christ to suffer in order to enter into his glory (v. 26-27). Not only did Jesus promise this (9:22, 44; 18:31-33), but it is the true meaning of "all the scriptures", beginning with Moses and the prophets (v. 27). The narrative has now reached another turning point. Initiative must come from the erring disciples themselves. Has the word of Jesus made any impact upon them? The original Greek of v. 28 means: "He pretended to be going further" (AT). The disciples must now take some initiative in response to Jesus' biblical catechesis. They do so generously: "Stay with us for it is toward evening, and the day is now far spent" (v. 29). A process of repentance and forgiveness is under way as Jesus walks with his fragile disciples.

At the meal the disciples recognise him in the breaking of the bread (vv. 30-31). The memory of the many meals that Jesus has shared with them, and especially the meal he shared on the night before he died (22:14-38), opens their eyes and anticipates the many meals that will be celebrated in the future. "That same hour they got up and returned to Jerusalem" (v. 33). The journey "away from Jerusalem" (v. 13) has been reversed as they turn back "to Jerusalem" (v. 33). Before they can even utter a word about their experience, they find that Easter faith is already alive. They are told: "The Lord has risen indeed and has appeared to Simon" (v. 34). Easter faith already has been born in Jerusalem, the city they should never have left.

As the Gospel opened, the audience met a fisherman called "Simon" (4:38). Within the context of a miraculous catch of fish he was called to be a disciple of Jesus and Jesus introduced a new name for him: "Peter" (5:8). From that point on, throughout the Gospel, he is called "Peter" (6:14; 8:45, 51; 9:20,

> As with the women (v. 4), so also with Peter (v. 12). His visit to the graveyard allows him to see what the women saw: an empty tomb, and the signs of what the Christian reader can recognise as God's victory over death. But an empty tomb only generates wonder about what it might mean. Easter faith is not born in a cemetery (vv. 3, 5, 12), but in remembering the words of Jesus (vv. 6-10).

Luke 24:36-49
Jesus Appears to His Disciples

36 While they were talking about this, Jesus himself stood among them and said to them, "Peace be with you."[a] 37 They were startled and terrified, and thought that they were seeing a ghost. 38 He said to them, "Why are you frightened, and why do doubts arise in your hearts? 39 Look at my hands and my feet; see that it is I myself. Touch me and see; for a ghost does not have flesh and bones as you see that I have." 40 And when he had said this, he showed them his hands and his feet.[b] 41 While in their joy they were disbelieving and still wondering, he said to them, "Have you anything here to eat?" 42 They gave him a piece of broiled fish, 43 and he took it and ate in their presence. 44 Then he said to them, "These are my words that I spoke to you while I was still with you—that everything written about me in the law of Moses, the prophets, and the psalms must be fulfilled." 45 Then he opened their minds to understand the scriptures, 46 and he said to them, "Thus it is written, that the Messiah[c] is to suffer and to rise from the dead on the third day, 47 and that repentance and forgiveness of sins is to be proclaimed in his name to all nations, beginning from Jerusalem. 48 You are witnesses[d] of these things. 49 And see, I am sending upon you what my Father promised; so stay here in the city until you have been clothed with power from on high."

28, 32-33; 12:41; 18:28). At the Last Supper he is still "Peter" (22:8, 34, 54, 55, 58, 60-61). Only in foretelling his future denials does Jesus revert to the name he had before he became a disciple: "Simon, Simon, listen! Satan demanded to sift all of you like wheat" (22:31). Yet, it is to the failed Simon that the risen Lord has appeared, to restore his apostolic role (24:34). At the end of the Emmaus story, as two failing disciples are returned to God's saving story, another sinner, Simon, has also been touched by the presence of the risen Lord (23:34). This unforgettable story conveys a powerful message: God has definitively established forgiveness of sin through the death and resurrection of Jesus.

Commissioning (vv. 36-49)

Jesus "stood among them" as they were discussing the events of Simon and the travellers to Emmaus. Jesus' greeting of peace generates fear. They think they are seeing a ghost (vv. 36-37). Consistent with all the Gospels, the appearance of the risen Jesus produces doubt and fear (Mark 16:8; Matt 28:17; John 20:1-2, 11-17, 24-29). Neither the vision of his hands and feet, nor his request that they touch him, can convince them that he is not a ghost (vv. 39-40). There is only one way to resolve this unfaith and amazement: celebrate a meal (vv. 41c-43) and remind them of his word and the fulfilment of the Scriptures (vv. 44-46).

> But another journey is about to begin, and the apostles return to Jerusalem, obedient to the command of Jesus (v. 49). In the midst of their fear and unfaith, the passion, death, resurrection, and ascension of Jesus have produced great joy among these founding figures, who will preach repentance and the forgiveness of sin, in Jesus' name, to the whole world (v. 52).

Jesus is with the apostles and disciples from this point on, until he leaves them in the ascension in v. 51. The meal-table is the place where he gives them his final instructions, based upon Scripture (v. 46), and commissions them to go to "all nations" (v. 47). He leads them to Bethany, blesses them, and is taken up into heaven (vv. 50-51). Only after the meal do the apostles demonstrate their faith. They worship him in Jerusalem (v. 52). All fear, doubt and amazement have disappeared.

There are close parallels between the experience of the Emmaus disciples and the experience of the eleven apostles: Jesus appears (vv. 15 and 36), he is not recognised (vv. 16 and 37), he instructs the disciples (vv. 27 and 44-49), a meal (vv. 30-31 and 41-42), Jesus disappears (vv. 31 and 51), and disciples return to Jerusalem (vv. 33 and 52).

At Emmaus (vv. 13-35) and in Jerusalem (vv. 36-52), post-resurrection meals close the many meals across the Gospel. Fulfilling Jesus' promise at the meal before his death, his sharing table with his disciples and apostles after his resurrection announces that the kingdom of God has come (22:14-23). At this final shared table, Jesus commissions his apostles to witness repentance and forgiveness of sins to all the nations (vv. 44-49). Jesus' suffering and death interrupted fellowship at table, but it has been re-established by his resurrection, as he promised in 22:16, 18.

A double dynamic is at work in Jesus' commission to the apostles. All that Jesus has said is the fulfilment of God's design, mapped out in the Law of Moses, the prophets and the psalms. The suffering, crucified and risen Christ has fulfilled God's design (vv. 44-46). They are thus witnesses and are to preach repentance and forgiveness of sins to all nations (v. 47). However, there is more to it. The two meal encounters in vv. 13-35 and vv. 36-43 highlight Jesus' presence to sinful disciples and apostles. On the basis *of their own experience of repentance and forgiveness of sins,* the apostles are commissioned to witness to all the nations (v. 47). The risen Jesus tells them to wait in the city of Jerusalem. There the power from on high will be given to them, and from Jerusalem they will set out to preach repentance and the forgiveness of sins in the name of Jesus (vv. 47-49). As followers of Jesus who have themselves sinned, they are eminently qualified to do so!

Ascension (vv. 50-53)

Jesus leads his disciples out to Bethany. Without a word, he raises his hands in blessing (v. 50). His journey began in Nazareth and will conclude in heaven, via the

events that have occurred in the city of Jerusalem. The journey from Galilee to Jerusalem was mapped out in 9:51-19:44. It comes to an end as he is carried up into heaven (24:51). But another journey is about to begin, and the apostles return to Jerusalem, obedient to the command of Jesus (v. 49). In the midst of their fear and unfaith, the passion, death, resurrection, and ascension of Jesus have produced great joy among these founding figures, who will preach repentance and the forgiveness of sin, in Jesus' name, to the whole world (v. 52).

To the ends of the earth

The Gospel ends where it began: in the Temple (1:5-24), as the apostles are continually in the courts of the Temple, praising God (v. 53). But so much has been said and done between the annunciation to Zechariah (1:5-24) and the continual praise of the apostles in the Temple (24:52-53). The apostles will soon be clothed with the power from on high (v. 49. Acts 2:1-4). The journey of the disciples is about to begin, driven by the Spirit and dominated by the journeys of Paul to the ends of the earth in Acts 13:1-28:31.

SUMMING UP

+ The Gospel of Luke and the Acts of the Apostles were written by the same author.

+ These two books tell the Christian story from the birth of Jesus until Paul's missionary presence in Rome via the paschal events and the gift of the Spirit in Jerusalem.

+ Luke shares only the account of the women at the empty tomb with the other Gospels, and only Luke reports the journey to Emmaus and Jesus' ascension.

+ Meals are very important in both the Gospel of Luke and the Acts of the Apostles. They are also important in Luke 24.

+ "Journeys" are important to both the Gospel of Luke and the Acts of the Apostles. They are also important in Luke 24.

Chapter Six
Two Stories in the Gospel of John

The Gospel of John dedicates two chapters to the discovery of an empty tomb and subsequent events. John 20 has long been regarded as the original final chapter to the Gospel. But we have already seen that John 21, even if added at a later date in the composition of the Gospel, has to be understood as a necessary epilogue to John's story of Jesus. We will consider John 20 and John 21 in distinct chapters, in order to convey the riches of the Johannine tradition.

John 20

The episodes reported in John 20 trace the faith response of some of Christianity's foundational characters: Peter and the Beloved Disciple (vv. 2-10), Mary Magdalene (vv. 11-18), the disciples as a group (vv. 19-23), and Thomas (vv. 24-29). In v. 29 Jesus blesses those who have not seen him, yet believe, and the account moves easily into John's final words in verses 30-31. John 20:1-31 traces the faith experience of the characters in the story and appeals to the faith of the audience.

✢ Mary Magdalene, Simon Peter and the Beloved Disciple (vv. 1-2).

✢ Simon Peter and the Beloved Disciple's journey of faith at the empty tomb (vv. 3-10).

✢ Mary Magdalene's encounter with the risen Jesus and her journey of faith (vv. 11-18).

✢ Jesus commissions the disciples and confers the Holy Spirit (vv. 19-23).

✢ Thomas' journey of faith (vv. 24-29)

✢ The First conclusion to the Gospel (vv. 30-31).

Mary Magdalene, Simon Peter and the Beloved Disciple (vv. 1-2)

John reports the presence of a single woman at the tomb: Mary Magdalene. She came there "on the first day of the week, while it was still dark" (v. 1). For John, darkness is an indication of a lack of faith (1:5). Unlike the first light of the other Gospels (Mark 16:2), Mary approaches in the darkness. She sees that the stone had been removed (v. 1) and rushes to Simon Peter and the other disciple, whom Jesus loves, to report to them that the tomb has been emptied by someone, and none of them knew where they have placed the executed Jesus.

She associates the two disciples ("we do not know") with her absence of Easter faith. Jesus' crucified body has been taken from the tomb.

Mary rightly intuits that a third person has entered the story: "someone" has entered the tomb (v. 2). There is no hint of belief in the action of God in the responses of Mary Magdalene, Simon Peter, and the other disciple, whom Jesus loved. All three are at a stage of non-belief (v. 2: "we do not know").

The Beloved Disciple's Journey of Faith (vv. 3-10)

Mary Magdalene has run *away from* the tomb in order to report her unfaith to the two disciples. Simon Peter and the other disciple reverse that flight. They run *to* the tomb (v. 3). This is already a sign of a more positive response. Peter leads in the run to the tomb, but the other disciple passes him. This unnamed disciple, whom Jesus loved (v. 2), is moving toward belief (v. 4), but he waits at the entry to the tomb to give first access to Peter (v. 5). To this point nothing has been said about the faith of the two disciples, but the signs are promising. Moving away from the negative witness of Mary Magdalene, they are at the tomb.

Simon Peter bends down and looks into the tomb. He sees that the cloths of death are empty. They

---

John 20:11-18
Jesus Appears to Mary Magdalene

11 But Mary stood weeping outside the tomb. As she wept, she bent over to look[a]into the tomb; 12 and she saw two angels in white, sitting where the body of Jesus had been lying, one at the head and the other at the feet. 13 They said to her, "Woman, why are you weeping?" She said to them, "They have taken away my Lord, and I do not know where they have laid him." 14 When she had said this, she turned around and saw Jesus standing there, but she did not know that it was Jesus. 15 Jesus said to her, "Woman, why are you weeping? Whom are you looking for?" Supposing him to be the gardener, she said to him, "Sir, if you have carried him away, tell me where you have laid him, and I will take him away." 16 Jesus said to her, "Mary!" She turned and said to him in Hebrew,[b] "Rabbouni!" (which means Teacher). 17 Jesus said to her, "Do not hold on to me, because I have not yet ascended to the Father. But go to my brothers and say to them, 'I am ascending to my Father and your Father, to my God and your God.'" 18 Mary Magdalene went and announced to the disciples, "I have seen the Lord"; and she told them that he had said these things to her.

are not only empty, but someone has folded them and placed them in different locations: the cloth that had been on Jesus' head had been "rolled up in a place by itself" (vv. 6-7). After Simon Peter has looked into the tomb, the Beloved Disciple enters the tomb. He also sees the signs of death; empty, folded, and placed. John declares that this disciple "saw and believed." Peter's response is not recorded, so we must not judge him one way or the other. John has his own reasons for singling out the faith of the Beloved Disciple at this stage and not reporting the response of Simon Peter.

What must be noticed is that the Beloved Disciple believes, but he does not see the risen Jesus. He believes on the basis of the signs in the tomb of God's action in raising his Son: the cloths of death have been emptied, folded and laid apart.

John then comments: "For as yet they did not understand the scripture, that he must rise from the dead" (v. 9). This Gospel is the story of the incarnation of the Word of God (1:18). John wrote what he regarded as the conclusion to Sacred Scripture. But Simon Peter and the Beloved Disciple "as yet did not understand the scripture". It was impossible for them to know the Scripture of the Gospel of John, as they are "in the story" and not recipients of this Scripture. A time will come when they, and others – especially all those who believe without seeing (cf. v. 29) – will accept the Gospel as Scripture and believe that Jesus had to rise from the dead. The two disciples return to their homes (v. 10). One of the several reasons why the

> Mary rightly intuits that a third person has entered the story: "someone" has entered the tomb (v. 2). There is no hint of belief in the action of God in the responses of Mary Magdalene, Simon Peter, and the other disciple, whom Jesus loved. All three are at a stage of non-belief (v. 2: "we do not know").

Johannine community will add 21:1-25 to the Gospel is to allow these two disciples, especially Simon Peter, to complete their journeys of faith.

Mary Magdalene's Journey of Faith (vv. 11-18)

Mary Magdalene is at the tomb, weeping (v. 11). Her sorrow continues to show her lack of faith. Like the disciples, she bent over and looked into the tomb, but her experience is unique. She sees two angels, messengers of God. The angels ask why she is weeping, but she can only repeat what she has said to the disciples in v. 2: someone has taken away the body of Jesus, and she does not know where they have put it (v. 13). There is not the slightest glimmer of resurrection faith in Mary's response to an empty tomb. The same disposition of unfaith continues when Jesus appears. Jesus is described as "standing", indicating the presence of the risen one, but she did not recognise him. Jesus repeats the question of the angels about her weeping, but she thinks he is the gardener and again asks about the removal of the body and its current location (vv. 14-15).

However, once Jesus identifies Mary by name, she greets him as her Rabbi and wishes to cling to him, to restore the bodily relationship she had with him during his ministry. There is no recognition of Jesus' teaching on the "hour" of his glorification through death and resurrection and his promised return to his Father (vv. 16-17a; 11:4; 13:31-32; 12:28; 17:5).

Mary's attachment to Jesus is very *physical*. Jesus asks her to abandon such *conditioned faith* and announce the completion of the "hour" to his brethren: "But go to my brothers and say to them, 'I am ascending to my

Father and your Father, to my God and your God'" (v. 17). She responds without hesitation and announces to the assembled disciples, "I have seen the Lord" (v. 18). Mary Magdalene has completed her journey of faith, submitting without condition to the word of Jesus.

On the way, she has been called to abandon all attachment to the *physical reality* of the body of Jesus, as he is ascending to God. In doing so, she becomes "the apostle to the apostles".

Commissioning (vv. 19-23)

Jesus' words of explanation to Mary Magdalene indicate that his departure by means of ascension is imminent (v. 17), but before it takes place he commissions his disciples in vv. 19-23. Prepared by the Easter message from Mary Magdalene (v. 18), when the crucified and risen Jesus appears among them they are full of joy (vv. 19-20). However, unlike the Beloved Disciple (v. 8), they experience the *physical reality* of the Risen Lord: "He showed them his hands and his side. *Then* the disciples rejoiced when they saw the Lord" (v. 20). Seeing the crucified and risen Lord is the reason for their joy. They receive his peace and are told that as the Father had sent Jesus, so Jesus is now sending them (13:18-20; 17:18-19).

Given the importance of Jesus' promise in the discourse to give the disciples his "peace" (14:27 and 16:33), the peace-greeting of Jesus in 20:19, 21, 26 must be seen as a fulfilment of that promise. Full of the peace and joy generated by the "hour", they are to be his sent ones, the bearers of his word (18:21), and whoever receives them will receive Jesus and the one who sent him (13:20). John's audience will not have a physical experience of Jesus, but they will encounter the risen Lord in his disciples.

The commission of the disciples is further defined by a second gift of the Spirit and the command that they continue his critical presence in the world as they forgive and retain sin (vv. 22-23). Jesus' first gift of the Spirit is at the cross (19:30). The importance of this second gift is indicated by Jesus' breathing upon them, recalling the moment of creation in Genesis 2:7. The disciples who have received the command to love as Jesus loved them (13:34-35; 15:12, 17) continue to be gifted by his life-giving love. They receive his peace that produces joy (vv. 19-20); they are commissioned as sent ones of Jesus, just as he was the sent one of the Father (v. 21), and they receive the second gift of the Spirit as they are commissioned to repeat Jesus' judging presence in the world during his absence (vv. 22-23). Jesus has made visible the love of God on the cross, and by means of the cross and resurrection he will be glorified by returning to the Father and the glory that was his before the foundation of the world (11:4; 12:23, 27-28; 13:1; 17:1-5). He has loved and founded a Spirit-filled community of disciples, to whom he has made visible his crucified yet risen body (v. 20), and he has commissioned them to be his ongoing presence.

Thomas' Journey of Faith (vv. 24-29)

Initially, Thomas was not present when Jesus appeared to the disciples and commissioned them (v. 24).

He will not believe their confession of faith in the risen Jesus, unless Jesus fulfils certain physical conditions. Thomas must be able to see and touch the risen body (v. 25).

"A week later" Jesus comes

> Mary Magdalene has come to love, life and faith because she saw Jesus, and the same must be said of Thomas. Although there is no description of the disciples' journey from no faith to faith in the upper room, they rejoice and are commissioned because they have been shown the crucified and risen body of Jesus Christ (v. 20). But what of later generations of disciples who will never be shown the wounds of the living Christ, those who are reading and hearing this story of Jesus?

again, and Thomas is present. Jesus asks Thomas to perform his proof-ritual, but commands him to abandon his situation of "no faith" (vv. 26-27). Overcome, he makes his confession of faith: "My Lord and my God." (v. 28). Thomas has made a striking journey from absence (v. 24) to faith (v. 28) through a conditioned faith that insisted upon the *physical reality* of the body of Jesus (v. 25).

Mary Magdalene has come to love, life and faith because she saw Jesus, and the same must be said of Thomas. Although there is no description of the disciples' journey from no faith to faith in the upper room, they rejoice and are commissioned because they have been shown the crucified and risen body of Jesus Christ (v. 20). But what of later generations of disciples who will never be shown the wounds of the living Christ, those who are reading and hearing this story of Jesus?

It is at this point that Jesus says his final words in the original Gospel. They are directed to Thomas, but they look beyond the people in the Gospel story.

Jesus blesses future generations: "Have you believed because you have seen me? Blessed are those who have not seen and yet believe" (v. 29).

Across 20:1-29 female and male foundational disciples lack belief. Mary Magdalene cannot imagine resurrection as the explanation of an empty tomb (20:1-2, 11-15), Peter and the Beloved Disciple run to the tomb in puzzlement and perhaps hope (vv. 3-7), the disciples rejoice when they see Jesus' hands and side (v. 20). Thomas will only believe if he is granted a physical experience of Jesus' crucified and risen body (vv. 24-29). Mary Magdalene is led to belief in the risen Lord by means of an appearance, a desire to touch, and a commission (vv. 16-18); the disciples are blessed with the proclamation of Mary Magdalene (v. 18), the sight of the risen body, and Jesus' commissioning of them for the mission (vv. 22-23). Thomas believes in Jesus as Lord and God by

> What must be noticed is that the Beloved Disciple believes, *but he does not see the risen Jesus*. He believes on the basis of the signs in the tomb of God's action in raising his Son: the cloths of death have been emptied, folded and laid apart.

means of an appearance, a desire to touch, and a challenge (vv. 26-29). In this procession of faith-experiences, the Beloved Disciple stands out. John tells his audience that he saw and believed, but he did not see the risen Jesus, nor does he seek physical confirmation of a risen body (v. 8).

The first conclusion to the Gospel (vv. 30-31)

Seamlessly, the original Gospel closes by explaining the blessedness of those who, like the Beloved Disciple, believe without seeing (vv. 30-31). Looking back across the faith journeys recorded in the episodes of the Beloved Disciple, Mary Magdalene and Thomas, there is an important link between Jesus' final blessing of those who do not see and yet believe, and the experience of the Beloved Disciple: he did not see, and yet he believed (v. 8). This is what it means to be a beloved disciple. John suggests that later generations, those who do not see and yet believe (v. 29), have an advantage. In verses 30-31, in the light of verse 9, John explains why such is the case.

They have been provided with a "Scripture" that Simon Peter and the Beloved Disciple did "not yet know" (v. 9). Jesus did many signs, but they have not been *written* in this book (v. 30). John explains to his audience, at the end of the experience of this Gospel, that there is a purpose behind selection of the "signs" that were included in the story. What has been written was: "so that you (later generations of disciples who have not seen, but have this Gospel, this 'writing') may go on believing that Jesus is the Christ, the Son of God, and that believing you may have life in his name" (v. 31: AT). This was not yet available for Simon Peter and the Beloved Disciple (v. 9). But it is in the hands of those who are reading John's story of Jesus and in the ears and hearts of those who are hearing it.

Believing without seeing

The Beloved Disciple believed without seeing Jesus, but he did not yet have the Scripture (vv. 8-9). All subsequent disciples are to become beloved disciples, also believing without seeing, but having the Scripture of the Gospel of John in hand. John is concerned that the members of the post-Easter audience should believe. He sets the Beloved Disciple before them as the first example to follow. His kind of faith will be commended by the risen Jesus in v. 29. It is through loving disciples whose story is told in the Gospel of John that the love and the life of the crucified and risen Jesus Christ will be made visible, experienced by those who hear of Jesus through their word (17:20-23).

A Major Feast Day for Mary Magdalene

Mary Magdalene plays a key role in all Four Gospels as a major figure at the Cross (Mark 15:40; Matt 27:56; Luke 23:50; John 19:25), the burial (Mark 15:47; Matt 27:61; Luke 23:55 [see 8:1-3]), and at the tomb on Easter morning (Mark 16:1; Matt 28:1; Luke 24:10). In the Gospel of John, she is the only person who goes to the tomb. In all Gospels the women are commanded to proclaim the action of God in Jesus' resurrection. For his own reasons, Mark has them run away in fear (Mark 16:8), but they become the first witnesses to the resurrection in Matthew (28:10) and Luke (24:10).

The Gospel of John, doubtless closer to what took place that morning, follows Mary's struggle to let go of her blindness and prejudices. She accepts Jesus' commission: "Go to my brothers and say to them, 'I am ascending to my Father and your Father, to my God and your God.'" Without hesitation she announced: "I have seen the Lord" (John 20:17-18). Mary Magdalene became The Apostle of the Apostles, a Gospel-based expression used by Popes Paul VI and John Paul II to describe this unique woman from the dawn of Christianity.

Why have we not heard this before? In the Western Church, the Gospel portrait of Mary was lost by associating her with every "Mary" in the New Testament, and especially with the anonymous sinful woman who anoints Jesus' feet in Luke 7:36-50. Entirely without historical or Gospel support, this misogynist view dominated Western imagination, poetry, art, theatre, and music. It has generated an almost universal belief that Mary Magdalene was the morally corrupt woman of Luke 7:36-50. This view is beautifully (but wrongly) captured in The Last Temptation of Christ.

Pope Francis has formally corrected this false understanding. On June 3, 2016, the Holy Father raised the liturgical celebration of Saint Mary Magdalene from a memorial to a major Feast. She is to be celebrated, not as a sinner, for which there is no evidence, but as The Apostle of the Apostles, who must be solemnly "remembered" in the Liturgy every year. Her unique role in the story of God's action among us in and through his Son has been fittingly recognised.

SUMMING UP

+ There are two resurrection chapters in the Gospel of John.

+ John 20 continues the tradition of the empty tomb, but is more interested in presenting the faith journey of major characters from the earliest Church.

+ John regards his story of Jesus as bringing Scripture to its conclusion.

+ He is critical of those who come to believe only on the basis of the physical experience of Jesus.

+ Jesus praises and blesses those who, like the Beloved Disciple, believe without seeing.

+ John has written his Gospel to make such belief possible for later Christians who do not see Jesus.

JOHN 21

John 21:1-14
Jesus Appears to Seven Disciples

21 After these things Jesus showed himself again to the disciples by the Sea of Tiberias; and he showed himself in this way. 2 Gathered there together were Simon Peter, Thomas called the Twin,[a] Nathanael of Cana in Galilee, the sons of Zebedee, and two others of his disciples. 3 Simon Peter said to them, "I am going fishing." They said to him, "We will go with you." They went out and got into the boat, but that night they caught nothing.
4 Just after daybreak, Jesus stood on the beach; but the disciples did not know that it was Jesus. 5 Jesus said to them, "Children, you have no fish, have you?" They answered him, "No." 6 He said to them, "Cast the net to the right side of the boat, and you will find some." So they cast it, and now they were not able to haul it in because there were so many fish. 7 That disciple whom Jesus loved said to Peter, "It is the Lord!" When Simon Peter heard that it was the Lord, he put on some clothes, for he was naked, and jumped into the sea. 8 But the other disciples came in the boat, dragging the net full of fish, for they were not far from the land, only about a hundred yards[b] off. 9 When they had gone ashore, they saw a charcoal fire there, with fish on it, and bread. 10 Jesus said to them, "Bring some of the fish that you have just caught." 11 So Simon Peter went aboard and hauled the net ashore, full of large fish, a hundred fifty-three of them; and though there were so many, the net was not torn. 12 Jesus said to them, "Come and have breakfast." Now none of the disciples dared to ask him, "Who are you?" because they knew it was the Lord. 13 Jesus came and took the bread and gave it to them, and did the same with the fish. 14 This was now the third time that Jesus appeared to the disciples after he was raised from the dead.

John's story of Jesus left some crucial issues unresolved, especially as regards the inner-workings of the community of faith and love founded at the cross (19:25-27). Who belongs to this community? Another tension that emerged from the Gospel was the relationship between the Beloved Disciple and Peter. What was their role, and how was their authority to be exercised? John's second resurrection story faces issues arising in the post-Easter Johannine community. The narrative of John 21:1-25 unfolds in three sections.

+ Jesus' appearance and the miraculous catch of fish in Galilee (vv. 1-14).

+ Peter and the Beloved Disciple (vv. 15-24).

+ Second conclusion to the Gospel (v. 25).

A Fishing Miracle (vv. 1-14)

The account opens with a laconic statement that the Lord again revealed himself (v. 1). Five named and two unnamed disciples are mentioned. Although he appears in v. 7, there is no mention of the Beloved Disciple. A decision is made to set out on a fishing trip (v. 3).

The remarkable events that have dominated Simon Peter's life since his call, and Jesus' words of promise in 1:42, appear to have been forgotten as he announces, "I am going fishing" (v. 3).

After a fruitless night of fishing, Jesus stands on the beach "just as day was breaking," but the disciples are unable to recognise him (vv. 3-4). Jesus initiates contact, addressing them as "children", a form of address indicating intimate relationship (v. 5). He commands them to cast the net on the right side of the boat, promising that they will find fish (v. 6a). The obedient response of the disciples to Jesus' command bears abundant fruit (v. 6b).

The two disciples who played such an important role at the empty tomb, Peter and the Beloved Disciple (20:3-10), assume leading roles. The Beloved Disciple recognises the risen Jesus and tells Peter, but not the other disciples: "It is the Lord" (v. 7). As throughout the latter half of the Gospel, the Beloved Disciple and Simon Peter are "paired" (13:23-24; 18:15-16; 20:2-10). Peter adjusts his scant clothing and leaps into the water. The other disciples bring the boat to land, dragging the net with them (v. 8). They serve to round off this part of the story, bringing the

> The remarkable events that have dominated Simon Peter's life since his call, and Jesus' words of promise in 1:42, appear to have been forgotten as he announces, "I am going fishing" (v. 3).

boat and the fish to join Peter and Jesus on the shore.

A meal has been prepared: a charcoal fire with fish lying on it, and bread (v. 9). Peter's restoration is underway. He had earlier joined those who had gone out to arrest Jesus with lanterns and torches by a charcoal fire (18:3, 18). He is now invited to join Jesus at a meal prepared on another charcoal fire (21:9). Peter responds to Jesus' instruction to bring some of the fish that were caught (v. 10). He hauls the net ashore, undamaged despite the catch of 153 fish (v. 11).

It is impossible to summarise the many suggestions that have been made over the centuries to explain the number of the 153 large fish. No doubt the author had good reason for choosing the number 153, and it is possible that John may have used this figure because he had heard that there were exactly 153 fish in the net. It is not exactly an overwhelming number of fish to catch in a net.

The point, however, is that Jesus has worked a miracle, the result of which is a large number of fish, which should have torn the net (v. 11b). The seamless garment, a symbol of the Church, which could not be torn apart at the crucifixion of Jesus, is in John's mind (19:23-24). The universality of the Christian community, the result of the initiative of Jesus (v. 6), the leadership of the Beloved Disciple and Simon Peter (vv. 7, 10-11), and the participation of the disciples in the mission (4:34-38; 13:18-20; 17:18; 20:22), are the point of the story. The community generated by the risen Jesus will not be torn apart.

Jesus commands the disciples to eat the first meal of the day. There is a transformation of the disciples from verse 4, where they did not recognise Jesus. Guided by the faith of the Beloved Disciple and the actions of Simon Peter, they no longer dare query the identity of Jesus. They now recognise that the risen Lord is present (v. 7). In v. 9 a meal of fish and bread has been prepared. These elements recall the miracle of 6:1-15 where both bread and fish were multiplied to feed a multitude at Passover time. Within a universal community, gathered as the result of the initiative of the risen Christ, recognised as "the Lord" by the Beloved Disciple (v. 7) and under Simon Peter's leadership (vv. 8-9), the Eucharistic hints indicate a central act of Johannine worship (6:1-15, 51-58; 13:21-38; 19:34-35). This was the third time that the risen Jesus was revealed (v. 14).

Peter and the Beloved Disciple (vv. 15-24)

Continuing the previous narrative, "When they had finished breakfast" (v. 15a), John focuses upon the figure of Simon Peter. Jesus' thrice-repeated question asks Simon Peter to commit himself to love Jesus more than everything that has determined his life to this point: boats, nets, the catch, or anything else that might be self-serving (recall v. 3: "Simon Peter told them, 'I am going fishing.'"). With his opening question, "Do you love me more than these?" Jesus insists, despite Peter's displeasure, that Peter not fall back into his former life, during which he denied Jesus. Jesus' question begins a process which ultimately reconstitutes Peter. Peter responds unconditionally: his love for Jesus is known by the all-knowing risen Lord. On the basis of this response to his question, Jesus commands Peter to pasture his sheep. A relationship between the role of Peter and the role of Jesus the Good Shepherd in 10:14-18 is established. What is surprising, however, is that these same questions, answers, and imperatives are repeated three times (vv. 15-17). The major reason for Jesus' demanding a three-fold confession of love is Peter's three-fold denial of Jesus at the outset of the passion narrative (cf. 18:15-18, 25-27).

Peter has been close to Jesus throughout the ministry (cf. 1:40-42; 6:67-69; 13:6-10, 36-38; 18:15). This closeness was broken by his three-fold denial. But at the lifting up of Jesus on the cross (3:14; 8:28; 12:32), the Beloved Disciple remained a key figure (cf. 19:25-27). Both Peter and the Beloved Disciple rushed to the empty tomb (20:3-7). But, although the Beloved Disciples "saw and believed" (v. 8), they do not yet know the Scripture and return to their homes (vv. 9-10). This situation is overcome as Peter's honest protestations of love lead to the establishment of a new relationship: Jesus appoints Peter as the one who shepherds his sheep. As Jesus laid down his life for his sheep (10:15, 17, 18), so will Simon Peter. Although Peter does not yet know it, his ministry will cost him no less than everything (vv. 18-19).

Jesus reminds Peter of a time in the past, during the ministry of Jesus, when Peter showed a great deal of good will (6:67-69), but ultimately

> Both Peter (cf. vv. 18-19) and the Beloved Disciple (vv. 22-23) have died, but they have *both* been established by Jesus as foundational figures of a future community of disciples commanded to love as Jesus loved (13:34-35; 15:12, 17) – because of their love for Jesus (21:7, 15-17; 20).

went into denial (18:15-18, 25-27). That was the time when Peter was young, when he girded himself and went where he would (v. 18a). He has now overcome the scandal of his rejection of Jesus and has unconditionally committed himself to the way of the Good Shepherd (vv. 15-17). The time will come, "when you are old", when Peter will lay down his life for the sheep of Jesus that have been entrusted to his care. Another will gird him and carry him where he would prefer not to go. **The audience knows that Peter had already stretched out his hands, an executioner had girded him with a cross, and he had laid down his life for the flock of Jesus. Thus, Jesus asks Peter to follow him down this way (v. 19b). This "following" has a physical meaning, as Peter walks behind Jesus (v. 20a), but it also means an undeviating discipleship for the rest of his days. Like Jesus, he will glorify God by his death (v. 19; 11:4; 13:31-32).**

Peter "follows", but in doing so he turns and sees the Beloved Disciple, described as the one who had lain close to Jesus' breast and had been asked for the identity of the betrayer (13:23-25). He is also "following" (v. 20). These two figures, one whose love for Jesus has just been re-established (vv. 15-17) and the other whose love has never been in question (13:23-25; 19:25-27; 20:2-9), are paired as "followers" of Jesus, with all that this entails (vv. 18-19). Peter asks: "Lord, what about this man?" (v. 21). Peter has been firmly established as a disciple and a pastor as a result of his loving commitment to Jesus (vv. 15-17). Questions remain around his relationship with the figure of the Beloved Disciple.

The paths of these two characters have been entwined across the latter part of the Gospel, at the last meal (13:23-25), in the court of the high priest (18:15-16), and at the empty tomb (20:3-10). On those occasions, despite Peter's obvious importance, the Beloved Disciple held pride of place (13:23; 18:15-16; 20:4, 8). Peter denied his association with Jesus (18:17-18, 25-27), while the Beloved Disciple was with the Mother of Jesus at the cross, and "because of that hour" took her to his own home (19:25-27). He was the only one reported to have come to faith at the empty tomb (20:8). The community whose Jesus-story is found in the Gospel of John regarded the Beloved Disciple as their founding figure (19:25-27).

However, if the story has reported that Peter was appointed disciple and pastor of the community as a result of his love for Jesus (vv. 15-17), not only Peter *in the story* but also *the readers and hearers of the Gospel* might ask: "What about this man?" (v. 21). Has this second resurrection story relegated the Beloved Disciple to a role of lesser significance than the one that he assumed in the earlier parts of the Gospel, especially as the son of the Mother of Jesus in 19:25-27?

The community thought that Jesus had said the Beloved Disciple would remain until his final return (v. 22), but that calls for correction (v. 23). What was central to Jesus' words, comments John, is: "*If it is my will.*" Jesus did not say that the Beloved Disciple would not die before the coming of Jesus, but that his future would be determined by the will of Jesus (vv. 22, 24). The death of the Beloved Disciple is the problem behind this clarification of what exactly Jesus had said. "The saying spread abroad … that this disciple was not to die" (v. 23a). But "this saying", this expression of popular opinion, was based on a faulty understanding of Jesus' earlier words. The Beloved Disciple is no longer alive, and the community should not wonder at his death. Whatever has happened to the Beloved Disciple is the fulfilment of Jesus' design.

Both Peter (cf. vv. 18-19) and the Beloved Disciple (vv. 22-23) have died, but they have both been established by Jesus as foundational figures of a future community of disciples commanded to love as Jesus loved (13:34-35; 15:12, 17) – because of their love for Jesus (21:7, 15-17; 20).

The community that received this Gospel lived in a time after the death and departure of Jesus, and after the deaths of Simon Peter and the Beloved Disciple. The narrator, therefore, has more to say about the Beloved Disciple. The Beloved Disciple is the author of the community's story of the life and teaching, death and resurrection of Jesus (v. 24). As John has said earlier in the story: "we know that his testimony is true" (19:35).

Living in the in-between-time, after the death and departure of Jesus, and the deaths of Peter and

> Living in the in-between-time, after the death and departure of Jesus, and the deaths of Peter and the Beloved Disciple, awaiting Jesus' return, the community has a link between the events of the past and the experience of the present provided by the Beloved Disciple's witness. He was a disciple of Jesus who both witnessed "these things", and then became the author of a record which transmitted "these things". The community can be confident of the truth of their story of Jesus and their commitment to love as Jesus has loved (13:34-35; 15:12, 17).

The audience knows that Peter had already stretched out his hands, an executioner had girded him with a cross, and he had laid down his life for the flock of Jesus. Thus, Jesus asks Peter to follow him down this way (v. 19b). This "following" has a physical meaning, as Peter walks behind Jesus (v. 20a), but it also means an undeviating discipleship for the rest of his days. Like Jesus, he will glorify God by his death (v. 19; 11:4; 13:31-32).

the Beloved Disciple, awaiting Jesus' return, the community has a link between the events of the past and the experience of the present provided by the Beloved Disciple's witness. He was a disciple of Jesus who both witnessed "these things", and then became the author of a record which transmitted "these things". The community can be confident of the truth of their story of Jesus and their commitment to love as Jesus has loved (13:34-35; 15:12, 17).

John's Second Conclusion (v. 25)

The Gospel comes to a second conclusion in a way that parallels the original conclusion of 20:30-31. John indicates that much more could have been written. Imitating other writers of the period (Eccles 12:9-12), he makes a different point. While 20:30-31 tell the audience *why* the Gospel has been written, 21:25 also points out that the story the audience has just read or heard has not exhausted all that could be said about Jesus (20: 30). They must look beyond the written pages of this book. Nothing written could tell the whole story.

A new commandment

In John 21 a very significant Christian tradition has its beginnings. Peter is the appointed shepherd of the flock, called to love to the point of death (cf. vv. 15-19), while the Beloved Disciple is the bearer of the authentic Jesus-tradition (v. 24). Both are crucial to a community of disciples called to love as Jesus loved. But the two ministries are distinguished. Considering the story of the entire Gospel, there can be little doubt that the Beloved Disciple is the most significant disciple. However, Peter is also called to service and death, restored to love of Jesus. The ministry of the Beloved Disciple has been to witness to Jesus in a way that goes on generating life and love because of what he has written. The ministry of Peter is to shepherd the flock.

The former is the more charismatic role of witnessing, the latter is the difficult task of governing and caring for the flock. Both are essential. The love shown in the witnessing of the Beloved Disciple, and the love shown in the service unto death of Simon Peter are the bedrock upon which all subsequent Johannine disciples might attempt to respond to the commandment of Jesus: "A new commandment I give to you, that you love one another; even as I have loved you, that you also love one another. By this everyone will know that you are my disciples, if you have love for one another" (13:34-35).

SUMMING UP

✛ John 21 should not be overlooked, even though there is a genuine conclusion to the Gospel of John in 20:30-31.

✛ It is often said that John 21 is about "Church order": who belongs to the community, and who are its authorities.

✛ Everyone can be caught into the net of the Church, and there is no fear that it will ever be torn apart.

✛ The early Christian tradition of Peter as the pastor and shepherd of the community is affirmed in the Gospel of John.

✛ The authority of the Beloved Disciple comes from having given the Church a living Word in his Gospel.

✛ Peter is the authority. The Beloved Disciple is the model disciple. The Church needs both: a loving leadership and a discipleship marked by love.

Chapter Seven
What Happened?

It is inevitable that we ask the question "what happened?" There is ample proof, even from non-Christian sources, that Jesus of Nazareth was crucified. The Christians believed that his death and burial were not the end, even if that meant ridicule from the world around them (1 Cor 1:22-25). As we have seen, the resurrection narratives show all the signs of the rich and faith-filled creativity of later writing, reading, and listening Christian communities.

There are no documented incidences of the resurrection from the tomb of a person who was certainly dead. There are no scientifically controllable criteria to judge with certainty what was said to the women at the tomb in the Easter proclamations and the exact nature of Jesus' appearances. Paul and the four Evangelists tell their stories of Jesus' death and resurrection in their own way. But it might be possible to trace solid evidence that one "fact" was not be shaped by the storytellers: Jesus was crucified and was laid in a tomb. After three days that tomb was found empty (Mark 16:1-5; Matt 28:1-6; Luke 24:1-3; John 20:1-2).

The Empty Tomb

Empty tombs generate fear, wonder and even flight (Mark 16:8; Matt 28:1-5; Luke 24:1-3; John 20:11-17). Charlie Chaplin died on Christmas Day, 1977. He was buried shortly after in the village cemetery Corsier-sur-Veve, near Lausanne, Switzerland. Two months later his grave was found empty. There was no outcry from Switzerland that

> If all the Gospels have women as the first witnesses to an empty tomb, they do so because that is what happened.

Charlie Chaplin had risen from the dead! His body had been stolen, and eventually the perpetrators were found and the body restored to a more secure grave. Empty tombs are not "good news", as someone has tampered with the remains of a deceased loved one. These sentiments lie behind all the Gospel accounts of the women's sad but loving journey to the tomb (Mark 16:1-2; Matt 28:1; Luke 24:1-3; John 20:1-2).

An empty tomb may not generate Easter faith, but it is an essential pre-requisite for the early Christian conviction that God had raised Jesus from the dead. Our reflection on the Pauline confession of faith in the death, burial, resurrection and appearances of Jesus took us back to the very dawn of Christianity (1 Cor 15:3-8). The story of a death, a tomb, and subsequent appearances was part of the Christian story well before the Gospels were written. The fact of an empty tomb is also supported by the presence of women as the witnesses in all the Gospels. Most likely, the Johannine account of Mary Magdalene at the tomb early on the Sunday morning reflects the oldest tradition. Within the Jewish world (and indeed elsewhere at the time), the witness of women was valueless, but the witness of only one woman was even worse.

If all the Gospels have women as the first witnesses to an empty tomb, they do so because that is what happened.

The empty tomb of Jesus, like the empty tomb of Charlie Chaplin, is not "good news". Precisely because this is the case, there was an empty tomb.

The earliest Christians did not come to faith because of an empty tomb. However, the fact of an

> The resurrection narratives show all the signs of the rich and faith-filled creativity of later writing, reading, and listening Christian communities.

empty tomb throws light upon the appearances.

This is the crucial issue. In several places in the Gospels, Jesus establishes, in encounters with his disciples, that the risen one they now acclaim as Lord is the same as the Jesus they knew during his life and ministry. This is the point of the resumed meals in the Lukan and the Johannine traditions (Luke 24:28-31; 41-43; John 21:9-14), and the presentation of his wounded body to his disciples in Luke (24:39-40) and to the disciples and Thomas in John (20:20, 24-29).

The Appearances

It is impossible to describe what actually happened in the post-resurrection appearances. We simply have no parameters with which we can judge what might have happened when someone who was crucified and buried appeared to women (all the Gospels), to two disciples on the road to Emmaus (Luke 24:13-35), to Peter (1 Cor 15:5; Luke 24:34), to a variety of gatherings of the disciples (1 Cor 15:6-8; Matt 28:16-20; Luke 24:35-53; John 20:19-23; 21:4-23), to the Twelve, to the more than five hundred, to James, to all the Apostles, and to Paul (1 Cor 15:5-9).

How can we decide whether or not Jesus suddenly appeared in locked rooms (Luke 24:36; John 20:19, 26), or describe what sort of "risen body" the women and the disciples actually "saw"? We cannot find anything from measurable human experience that enables us to affirm what actually happened.

God is at work

One thing is certain: the witness of the earliest Church that Jesus "appeared". We are not in a situation to describe the nature of these encounters, but that they took place should not be questioned. *What* took place is difficult to determine, but *that* they took place is affirmed by Paul, Mark, Matthew, Luke, John, and many other New Testament and earliest Christian witnesses. As we have seen, a passive form of the verb appears very often. Scholars call these verbs examples of the divine passive: God is at work. The earliest Church had no hesitation in affirming "the primacy of the divine initiative". That initiative cannot be measured.

Once this is accepted, we are moving away from the realm of controllable human experience to the realm of the inbreak of the divine into the human. We are invited to understand what the New Testament narratives wanted to say about God's action in and through the death and resurrection of his Son. These events took place, and the witness of the Christian Church and its subsequent traditions exist because of them. As believing Christians, we accept that there is no "knock-down" historical proof for the resurrection events reported in the Gospel narratives. But there is clear evidence that the earliest Church came into existence because of its encounters with the risen Jesus – whatever that means. Equally clear is the fact that Jesus of Nazareth was now their risen Lord.

SUMMING UP

✝ *Belief* generated by an empty tomb and appearances of the risen Jesus is witnessed from the earliest days of the Christian Church.

✝ An empty tomb does not generate Easter faith, but creates flight and fear. But it is an essential pre-requisite for Easter faith.

✝ The universal affirmation that the empty tomb was discovered by women (or maybe only Mary Magdalene) supports that "on the third day" Jesus' tomb was found empty.

✝ It is impossible to determine the nature of the appearances. That they took place is essential for the birth of the Christian Church.

Chapter Eight
What does the Resurrection of Jesus mean?

The earliest Christian tradition never debated what happened at the resurrection. Their concern was to communicate what the event meant. They identified what God did for Jesus, and what the risen Jesus does for his followers.

For Jesus

The belief that the action of God lies behind the resurrection of Jesus is found across all four Gospels. This is clearly seen in the series of passive verbs, indications of the action of God, in the resurrection narratives. The stone *has been rolled back* (Mark 16:4) or *was rolled back* by an angel of the Lord (Matt 28:2). As with the earliest Christian confessions (1 Cor 15:4), the Easter message to the women announces: "He *has been raised* (by God)" (Mark 16:6; Matt 28:6).

The beloved Son has not been abandoned by God; his unconditional acceptance of all that has been asked of him by the God whom he called "Father" (Mark 14:36; Matt 26:39) has been accepted as his Father enters the realms of death and raises his Son to life. Jesus' unconditional "yes" to God is now responded to by God's unconditional "yes" to Jesus (Rom 5:12-21). This fulfills the Scriptures, bringing God's design for Jesus to its conclusion. The Christ *must* suffer these things, and thus enter into his glory (Luke 24:26-27, 44-46). There is no point in seeking Jesus among the dead (v. 5).

Jesus of Nazareth would never accept a messianic acclamation that is not clarified by his role as the Son of Man who must suffer, die and be raised on the third day (Mark 8:31; 9:31; 10:32-34). On the walk to Emmaus the risen Jesus accuses the disciples of being foolish and slow of heart: "'Was it not necessary that *the Christ* should suffer these things and enter into his glory?' And beginning with Moses and all the prophets, he interpreted to them all the Scriptures concerning himself" (Luke 24:25-27). John states that he has told them this story so that his audience may

> The beloved Son has not been abandoned by God; his unconditional acceptance of all that has been asked of him by the God whom he called "Father" (Mark 14:36; Matt 26:39) has been accepted as his Father enters the realms of death and raises his Son to life. Jesus' unconditional "yes" to God is now responded to by God's unconditional "yes" to Jesus (Rom 5:12-21).

believe in the name of Jesus, the Christ, the Son of God, and thus have life in his name (20:30-31). It is as the crucified, risen and glorified Christ that Jesus gives eternal life. It is against this background that one can best understand the earliest Church's confession of Jesus as "Lord" (Rom 1:3-4; John 20:2, 13, 15, 18, 20, 25, 28; 21: 7 [twice], 12, 15, 16, 17, 20, 21). The resurrection of Jesus brings his God-given mission to an end and initiates the mission of his followers (1 Cor 15:5-8; Mark 16:7-8; Matt 28:16-20; Luke 24:44-40; John 20:1-21:25). He returns to the glory which was his before the foundation of the world (John 17:5). Every knee shall bow and tongue confess that Jesus Christ is Lord (Phil 2:11).

For Jesus' Followers

One of the most encouraging features of the Gospel stories is the realistic portrayal of fragile disciples. Stories of disciples who struggle to respond to Jesus' demands, found in all four Gospels, reflected the lived experience of the earliest Christians. Paul captured it in his exhortation, based on his own experience, to the Corinthians:

> "For the sake of Christ, then, I am content with weaknesses, insults, hardships, persecutions and calamities; for when I am weak, then I am strong" (2 Cor 12:10; 13:4).

It is this experience that has been captured in the Gospels' portrayal of the Gospels, a portrait that continues to the end of each story.

In all the Gospels, failing disciples are reconstituted, even though to the very end "some doubted" (Matt 28:17). Mark's enigmatic failure of the women in 16:8, the journey away from Jesus by Cleopas and his companion (Luke 24:13-35), and John's dramatic portrayal of the faltering faith of Mary Magdalene (John 20:11-18), Thomas (20:24-29), and Jesus' demand that Peter, the denier, confess his love three times (21:15-18), continue this theme. Forgiveness is implied by the commissioning of sinful disciples (Mark 16:7; Matt 28:16-20; Luke 24:46-49; John 20:22-23). The resurrection accounts not only tell of Jesus' vindication by God, but also the rehabilitation of sinful disciples. Despite Mary Magdalene, Thomas, and Simon Peter, John insists that the disciples are to continue the mission of Jesus (John 20:22-23). Their message will bring eternal life to those who have not seen, yet believe (20:29-31).

Finally, the risen and departing Jesus promises and gives his Spirit to his disciples to guide and strengthen them in his absence. In the Gospel of Luke, Jesus instructs his disciples: "And behold, I send the promise of my Father upon you; but stay in the city, until you are clothed with power from on high" (Luke 24:49). That "clothing" happens as the story of the early Church begins, on the first Christian Pentecost (Acts 2:1-4). In Jerusalem, people "from every nation" are present to hear the disciples speak in all the known languages, reversing the curse that began at the Tower of Babel. A new and universal people of God has been founded at a new Pentecost (Acts 2:5-12). They are to baptise in the name of the Father, the Son, and the Holy Spirit (Matt 28:19).

In the Gospel of John, Jesus promises the gift of the Spirit Paraclete (7:37-39; 14:15-17, 26; 15:26-27; 16:7-11, 12-15) and gives it abundantly in his "hour," as he makes God known by bringing his task to its perfect accomplishment (19:30), and in his commission to the disciples so that they might continue his critical, revealing and judgment presence in his absence (20:21-23). The association of the gift of the Spirit with the risen and departing Jesus brings to closure the need for Jesus to remain with his infant community. He will be with them always in the gift of his Spirit. His God and Father is their God and their Father (Matt 1:23; 28:20; John 20:17-18).

We live in the faith

There are many "wonders" scattered across the Gospel stories. None of them surpass the beginning and the end of Jesus' story. Christians believe that God entered the human story in and through his Son, Jesus of Nazareth. It is right that we are unable to explain how the human presence of the divine in our history began and ended, even though we live in the faith that this happened, despite the fact that it escapes our human measurement. As believing Christians, we affirm our right to claim that in Jesus we have been granted sight of the glory of God (John 1:14).

The imaginative telling and re-telling of the story of Jesus' death and resurrection have provided the basis for two thousand years of Christian faith. It has developed and enriched the Church's thought, culture, and practice across the centuries.

Believers wonder at what God has done for Jesus, and rejoice in what Jesus does for us in and through the resurrection. This is especially true in our current era, when Christian institutions are under threat from many sides, including some oppressive aspects in contemporary Christian practice. The stories of the resurrection challenge these threats. They assure us that Jesus' promises come true, that our fears, doubts, failures and sins are overcome, as we are sent out again and again on mission, accompanied by the never-failing presence of the risen Jesus in the gift of his Spirit.

SUMMING UP

✦ It is not possible to describe exactly what happened at the resurrection of Jesus.

✦ The New Testament offers firm proof for the existence of an empty tomb.

✦ Rather than report what happened, the New Testament authors were most concerned to explain what it meant.

✦ They wanted to explain what it meant for Jesus.

✦ Even more importantly, they wanted to explain what it means for us.

Believers wonder at what God has done for Jesus, and rejoice in what Jesus does for us in and through the resurrection. This is especially true in our current era, when Christian institutions are under threat from many sides, including some oppressive aspects in contemporary Christian practice. The stories of the resurrection challenge these threats. They assure us that Jesus' promises come true, that our fears, doubts, failures and sins are overcome, as we are sent out again and again on mission, accompanied by the never-failing presence of the risen Jesus in the gift of his Spirit.

References

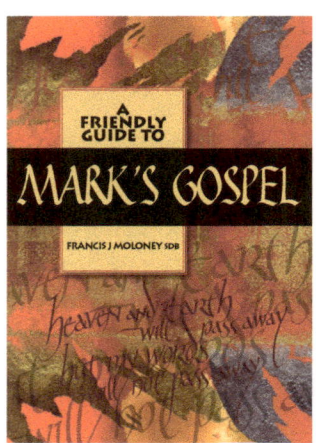

Allison, Dale C, *Resurrecting Jesus. The Earliest Christian Tradition and Its Interpreters* (New York/London: T. & T. Clark, 2005), 198-375.

O'Collins, Gerald, *Believing in the Resurrection. The Meaning and Promise of the Risen Jesus* (New York/Mahwah, NJ: Paulist, 2012).

Moloney, Francis J, *The Resurrection of the Messiah. A Narrative Commentary on the Resurrection Accounts in the Four Gospels* (Mahwah/New York:Paulist Press, 2013).

Moloney, Francis J, *A Friendly Guide to Mark's Gospel* (Mulgrave: Garratt Publishing, 2012).

Moloney, Francis J, *A Friendly Guide to The New Testament* (Mulgrave: Garratt Publishing, 2010).

Moloney, Francis J, *Reading the New Testament in the Church. A Primer for Pastors, Religious Educators, and Believers* (Mulgrave: Garratt Publishing, 2015).